GIFTE
TALENTED
from A-Z

Also available:

Teaching the Very Able Child Belle Wallace (1 85346 705 7)

Challenges in Primary Science David Coates and Helen Wilson (1 84312 013 5)

Curriculum Provision for the Gifted and Talented in the Primary School Deborah Eyre and Lynne McClure (1 85346 771 5)

Gifted and Talented Learners Barry Hymer and Deborah Michel (1 85346 955 6)

GIFTED AND
TALENTED
from A-Z

Jacquie Buttriss and Ann Callander

 David Fulton Publishers

In association with The National Association
for Able Children in Education

David Fulton Publishers Ltd
The Chiswick Centre, 414 Chiswick High Road, London W4 5TF

www.fultonpublishers.co.uk

First published in Great Britain in 2005 by David Fulton Publishers
10 9 8 7 6 5 4 3 2 1

Note: The right of Jacquie Buttriss and Ann Callander to be identified as the
authors of this work has been asserted by them in accordance with the Copyright,
Designs and Patents Act 1988.

David Fulton Publishers is a division of Granada Learning Limited, part of ITV
plc.

British Library Cataloguing in Publication Data
A catalogue record for this book is available from the British Library.

ISBN 1 84312 256 1

Typeset by Servis Filmsetting Ltd, Manchester
Printed and bound in Great Britain by Ashford Colour Press, Gosport

Contents

NACE National Office
PO Box 242
Arnolds Way
Oxford,
OX2 9FR
Tel: 01865 861879
Fax: 01865 861880

**National Association
for Able Children
in Education**

**NACE exists solely to support the daily work of teachers providing for
pupils with high ability, whilst enabling all pupils to flourish**

We are a large association of professionals. We deliver advice, training and
materials on learning and teaching; leadership and management; whole-school
improvement.

We provide:
• Specialist advice and information to teachers, LEAs and government agencies
• Courses, some in partnership with Granada Learning Professional
  Development and with optional online continuing support and access to tutors
• Bespoke courses and guidance delivered at your premises
• Tutors to work alongside teachers in the classroom
• Annual and regional conferences
• Market-leading books and seminal publications
• Keynote speakers for special events
• Support for special projects
• National and international links

Some of our most popular courses are linked to our best-selling books and
delivered by the author; an opportunity to really understand new strategies and
how to put them into practice.

Join us: membership gives you:
• Quick access to professional advice and resources
• Members' website, for updates and exchange of practice
• Termly newsletters, with practical articles and updates
• Biannual journals with more substantial articles relating research to practical
  strategies
• Discount on courses and conferences
• Access to network of members and regional groups

**Visit www.nace.co.uk
for list of publications, courses, services and to join NACE**

Advancing teaching: Inspiring able learners every day

Founded in 1984   Registered Charity No. 327230

Introduction

This book provides a comprehensive A–Z reference for everyone interested in gifted and talented education.

Those who work with gifted and talented children often know a great deal about some of the issues relating to their pupils' learning needs, but could do with a quick and easy look-up guide, covering all aspects of gifted and talented education. This A–Z glossary is intended to be just that, providing clear, user-friendly explanations of the terminology, theories and issues involved and how to find out more.

Gifted and Talented from A–Z will help you to answer specific questions such as:

- What do the words 'gifted' and 'talented' actually mean?
- Is there any support group I can recommend to the parents of a young gifted child?
- Who can I contact to give me some extension ideas for my maths students?
- I have heard a lot of talk about 'Accelerated Learning' – what is it?
- How can I find out about teaching philosophy in the classroom?
- What is the difference between 'enrichment' and 'extension'?
- Are there any practical books about how to teach thinking skills?
- Some of my students want to learn Latin – how can I make this possible for them?
- What are 'Multiple Intelligences' and where can I find out more about them?
- One of my pupils is mad keen on astronomy – what websites would you recommend?
- I am interested in doing some action-research – is there any funding available?
- What is the Challenge Award and how can I apply for it?

The answers to all these questions – and many more – are found within these pages. The gifted and talented education scene is changing and moving forward all the time, so it is especially important for all professionals involved in this field to have a handy and up-to-date reference guide.

In addition to the main A–Z text, there are cross-referenced sections on some of the principal researchers and theorists in gifted and talented education, the main organizations and support groups for parents and teachers, a selection of books and resources, their publishers and a range of useful websites, many of which have exciting interactive content to challenge and stimulate children, of all ages, from 2–95!

Throughout, our aim has been to provide our readers with a straightforward and user-friendly dip-in guide to the many issues and opportunities relating to the education of gifted and talented pupils. This book is by no means a complete answer to everything. Indeed, we hope it will raise more questions and that you will be able to find within its pages the appropriate sources to search for further answers.

A–Z Glossary of Gifted and Talented Education

A

Accelerated Learning

Accelerated Learning synthesises ideas about intelligence, thinking and learning and was developed by Colin Rose (see Who's Who) into teaching techniques for use in schools, drawing upon such areas of research as:

- the theory of Multiple Intelligences;
- preferred learning styles;
- creating a supportive learning environment;
- enhancing self-esteem;
- retaining and recalling information;
- enhancing memory and motivation.

The Accelerated Learning approach encompasses a belief that all learners can reach a level of achievement which may seem beyond them.

Accelerated learning cycle

This cycle provides a meaningful structure to the process of learning, but it is not meant to be a straitjacket for every learning opportunity. There are seven stages to the cycle:

- Stage One – Connect the learning. This involves giving children the opportunity to relate their previous learning to their present learning experience. It helps to identify what they have already learned and understood.
- Stage Two – The Big Picture. At this stage an overview of the lesson is given and key ideas and vocabulary are introduced.

- Stage Three – Describe the outcomes. It is important to share the lesson objectives with pupils, describing what should be achieved by the end of the lesson.
- Stage Four – Give the input. This involves giving children the opportunity to use their own preferred learning style, such as VAK – visual, auditory and kinaesthetic – styles of teaching and learning (see separate entries).
- Stage Five – Activity. The activity should incorporate the use of different intelligences, use interactive and collaborative learning experiences and provide a balance of VAK styles of learning.
- Stage Six – Demonstrate understanding. It is important that pupils are given opportunities to show their conceptual understanding of a topic throughout the lesson.
- Stage Seven – Review for recall and retention. There need to be regular review sessions during and at the end of each lesson. The ideal review cycle for recall and retention of information is: during the lesson – at the end of the lesson – within 24 hours – within one week – within one month – within six months – within one year.

Acceleration

Acceleration is the practice of arranging for pupils to work for all, or part of their time with pupils in a higher year group. If this cannot be arranged, acceleration can take the form of allowing children to work on curriculum materials designed for older pupils. When considering acceleration, it is important to make provision for the all-round development of children as well as making provision for the area in which they excel.

ACTS

ACTS is the acronym for Activating Children's Thinking Skills, a project which aims to promote the development of thinking skills in ordinary classrooms at Key Stage 2 by doing the following:

- using an infusion approach – infusing subject content with the teaching of relevant thinking skills in an explicit way;
- developing a thinking vocabulary through encouraging children to discuss, listen, question and reflect;
- using thinking diagrams to outline the sequence or pattern of an activity. This helps learners with decision-making and to understand the steps involved in thinking.

The initial project was directed by Dr Carol McGuinness and involved a group of teachers in Northern Ireland. Learning contexts were identified, then lessons developed where relevant thinking skills and subject understanding could be taught explicitly.

A

Advanced Extension Awards

These are tests specifically designed to challenge the most able 18-year-olds by requiring a greater depth of understanding, together with the ability to think critically at a level higher than is demanded by 'A' Levels.

Advanced Learning Centres

Advanced Learning Centres (ALCs) are an innovation pioneered and promoted by the National Primary Trust (NPT), that can organise training and co-ordinate funding. The first ALCs were in English (Advanced English Centres, or AECs) and maths (Advanced Maths Centres, or AMCs). These are now being extended to include centres focusing on ICT, Modern Languages, Drama, Art, Philosophy and Music. ALCs aim to cater for the needs of primary-aged children who show high aptitude in particular subjects or skills. ALCs usually take place after school or at weekends throughout the year, supporting children in their exploration and discovery of a subject and thereby enriching their learning experiences. More information about ALCs is available on the NPT website (see Organisations).

Aimhigher

This is a government initiative, which seeks to raise aspirations and improve access to higher education for young people from disadvantaged backgrounds. A key focus of the initiative is to provide advice and support for gifted and talented youngsters in the 14–19 age group. 'Strand One' of Aimhigher concentrates on meeting the needs of post-16 gifted and talented learners.

ALPS

The acronym for Accelerated Learning in Primary Schools, ALPS is an approach to learning, devised by Alistair Smith and Nicola Call, that draws upon research by Gardner (theory of Multiple Intelligences), Jensen (brain-based learning), Goleman (emotional intelligence) and Dennison (Brain Gym). The ALPS approach provides strategies for primary teachers using accelerated learning techniques.

Assessment

It is important to clarify the difference between assessment for the purposes of identification of gifts or talents (see Identification) and assessment of attainment, related to learning objectives, or progress related to prior attainment. The assessment of gifted and talented pupils' achievements is in many ways similar to the assessment of all pupils' work, except that it may prove to be more complicated for a non-specialist teacher to assess the attainment or progress of those pupils who have exceptional abilities in advanced subject areas. Assessment strategies for gifted and talented children fall into three main types:

- Teacher assessment, usually linked to planned learning objectives, National Curriculum level descriptions or to other specific criteria. (Since the demise of SATs extension tests in 2002, additional assessment tasks for more able pupils have been provided by the government to support teacher assessment in Key Stages 1–3 in English, Maths and Science.)
- Standardised tests, such as baseline profiles, National Curriculum Standard Assessment Tests conducted at the end of each key stage, optional QCA standardised tests, or CATs (Cognitive Ability Tests) which assess verbal and non-verbal skills and reasoning abilities.
- Self-assessment, which requires pupils to evaluate and reach judgements about their own progress, learning and achievements.

B

BACE

The Brunel Able Children's Education (BACE) Centre at Brunel University was Britain's first university-based research and teacher-support centre for gifted children. BACE has links with international centres in the USA and Australia. (See Organisations.)

Barriers to Learning

'Barriers to learning' is a term used in the 2001 SEN Code of Practice, to include a range of difficulties that may affect a child's ability to achieve his or her potential. Gifted and talented children may experience 'barriers to learning' that could include:

- physical disability;
- a diagnosed condition or syndrome;
- English as an additional language;
- chronic illness;
- adverse environmental influences.

Gifted or talented children who also have barriers to learning have what is known as double exceptionality (see separate entry).

B

Beacon schools

Beacon schools were established in 1998. Any type of state-maintained school, in England, could be part of the programme if they had been identified as a high performing school. The aim of the Beacon school programme was to help raise standards by sharing examples of successful practice through partnerships between schools. Beacon schools could use their additional funding to offer advice and set up networks for the dissemination of good practice across a wide range of areas, including provision for gifted and talented children. Beacon schools are gradually being phased out and this initiative has now been replaced by the Leading Edge Partnership: Leading Edge Schools (secondary) and Leading Practice Schools (primary) (see separate entries).

Behaviour

There are two main types of behaviour difficulties associated with giftedness. The first is that behaviour problems can sometimes mask underlying giftedness in the disaffected able pupil. There are many reasons why potential high-flyers may not reveal their abilities. Some innately gifted pupils may be under-challenged in their mainstream classrooms, thereby lacking outlets for their creative and intellectual capacities. This often results in either a sullen or withdrawn manner, or in disruptive and possibly confrontational behaviours. Conversely, it can be very difficult for a teacher to identify a pupil with a negative attitude, low self-esteem or anti-social behaviour as a potentially gifted child, so this is a complex 'vicious circle'. This may be further exacerbated if a pupil has a learning difficulty alongside his or her gift or talent, resulting in frustration, which in turn may cause negative behaviour patterns (see Double exceptionality).

The other type of behaviour which presents in some particularly gifted children is the type of alienation which may occur if the child feels in any way isolated by his or her giftedness. This may be helped by working on self-esteem, together with an understanding that being 'different' is not in any way negative or anti-social and that all children have different strengths and are, in their own ways, 'different'. This approach works most effectively as part of a positive whole-school policy.

Early identification of gifted or talented children is the ideal and should preclude – or at least minimise – the behavioural problems which might otherwise occur. But there is also a continuing need to raise self-esteem, so as to ensure the continuation of a positive attitude towards learning and achievement.

Bloom's taxonomy

In 1956, a group of educational psychologists, led by Benjamin Bloom, developed a classification system (a taxonomy) of educational objectives. Their findings were divided into three domains (cognitive, psychomotor and affective). There were six levels in the cognitive domain, six levels in the psychomotor domain and five levels in the affective domain. Each of these domains was classified into a hierarchy that has become known as Bloom's taxonomy. The cognitive domain has probably been the most widely used within an educational context and consists of:

- knowledge (recall and repeat information);
- comprehension (understand meaning, infer causes, predict consequences);
- application (apply knowledge in new situations or to solve problems);
- analysis (compare/contrast, categorise; cause/effect, fact/ opinion, relevant/irrelevant);
- synthesis (combine knowledge drawn from several areas into new ideas);
- evaluation (judge the value of materials and ideas, make comparisons in different situations, recognise subjectivity).

Bodily-kinaesthetic intelligence

See Multiple Intelligences.

Brain

Research into the workings of the brain has shown the tremendous capacity our brains have for learning. Some researchers believe that there are over 100 billion active neurons in our brain. Each one of these neurons is capable of making 20,000 connections with other brain cells. So the more we use our brains, the more connections we make. The connections that we make at a young age are our routes to learning as we go through life. A stimulating, challenging and fun environment influences the capacity that we have for making these connections.

Recent brain research has discovered that enhancing self-esteem and creating an emotionally supportive learning environment actually does have a biological effect on our brains. Brain scans have shown that when we are under stress the flow of blood is drawn away from the neo-cortex (the 80 per cent of our brain where higher order thinking occurs) to the 'reptilian brain' (the 5 per cent of our brain which controls routine body functions and survival responses). This also affects the limbic system-mid brain (the 15 per cent of our brain where our emotional responses, sense of self-identity, beliefs and values are located). A high level of motivation and self-esteem allows one to function more effectively as a learner. (See also 'Triune Brain'.)

Brain-based learning

Brain-based learning looks at how each person interprets and processes information in a unique way. The brain stores both our conscious and unconscious memories, so even our early learning experiences have an impact on our learning style preferences. Brain-based learning recognises that the learning process engages the whole person and that emotions affect the way that we learn. Negative emotions can act as barriers to learning, often leaving the emotion remembered rather than the learning. Enjoyment and the feeling of success are important elements of effective learning.

Brain breaks

Research suggests that physical movement increases the oxygen in the bloodstream and helps to improve concentration. Many children have difficulty sitting still for too long and need to be given opportunities to energise or relax their brains in order to enhance readiness for learning. Brain breaks can be:

- Simple physical activities to help refocus children's attention and concentration. These may be cross-lateral movements to support the development of both gross and fine motor control as well as hand–eye co-ordination;

- Physical activities to help children remember specific number facts (times tables), spellings, conceptual vocabulary, etc.;
- Role-play activities to help children understand and empathise with a different time or place such as in history or geography.

Brain Gym

Brain Gym is an educational movement-based programme using simple activities to integrate the whole brain, senses and body, enhancing a child's physical skills and increasing his concentration. It was devised by Dr Paul Dennison, following his research into brain function, to make brain and body connections which enhance:

- sensory integration;
- motor integration;
- emotional/behavioural balance;
- efficient body functioning.

The programme consists of 25 Brain Gym exercises, most of which are easily performed in the classroom. It is suggested that the time spent – usually only a few minutes at a time – results in increased concentration and efficiency, thereby enhancing teaching and learning. Sipping water is also an integral part of Brain Gym as it appears to increase memory and nerve functions.

C

CAGE (Cognitive Acceleration through Geography Education)

This is a cognitive acceleration programme developed to focus on Key Stage 3 pupils to enhance their thinking in order to extend and enrich their geography skills.

Cambridge School Classics Project, including online Latin

This project emerged from various research studies, which suggest that the learning of Latin contributes to students' intellectual and linguistic development. The Cambridge School Classics Project provides a number of options for pupils to study Latin – either in school or at home – either online or as a correspondence course. Various levels of support are available. Many mainstream schools across the UK have been able to secure DfES funding to help them set up projects within their schools, to access online Latin courses for their pupils. All ages can be catered for, but most of the funded projects have been for students in Years 7, 8 or 9 in mainstream secondary schools.

CAME (Cognitive Acceleration through Mathematics Education)

This is a cognitive acceleration programme aimed at developing Key Stage 3 pupils' ability to think mathematically. Each carefully structured lesson aims to challenge pupils' thinking through focused group and class discussion alongside adult mediation. The development of pupils' reasoning ability – through the use of metacognitive strategies – provides a foundation for the understanding of more advanced Maths later.

CASE (Cognitive Acceleration through Science Education)

The materials are designed to encourage young people, at Key Stage 3, to make use of metacognitive skills when solving Science problems. The course is designed to be taught over two years and has been successful in raising the standard of children's thinking. CASE teachers are trained to challenge pupils' current level of understanding and encourage them to explain and evaluate their problem-solving strategies in small group and class discussion (see Websites).

CATE (Cognitive Acceleration through Technology Education)

This is a similar project to those described above (CAGE, CAME and CASE), developing pupils' thinking skills to enhance their learning in all aspects of Technology.

CATS

See Cognitive ability tests.

Center for Talented Youth (CTY)

The highly respected Center for Talented Youth was founded at Johns Hopkins University, Maryland, USA, in 1979 and has been the inspiration for many national centres and academies worldwide, including our own National Academy for Gifted and Talented Youth (see separate entry). The CTY provides a comprehensive service ranging across all aspects of provision for gifted and talented youth, internationally. This includes a talent search, focusing on identification, a wide variety of summer schools across

C

the USA, online courses, information, counselling and advice, research, conferences and a magazine for gifted students. Distance learning provision includes academically challenging courses in writing, maths, ICT and physics, using online and CD resources, for use at school or at home.

Challenge Award

The Challenge Award is a valuable resource set up and administered by NACE (see Organisations) for the evaluation, accreditation, recognition and celebration of schools demonstrating quality whole-school provision for able, gifted and talented pupils. An integral aspect of this Challenge Award is the rigorous Self-Evaluation Framework (see separate entry). Schools can apply for the Challenge Award when they are able to demonstrate – from evidence gathered using the self-evaluation framework – that they meet the criteria of the ten elements which make up the award. The framework supports schools in developing quality provision – whatever their starting point – giving a clear structure, shape and direction for planning and action.

Challenge days

In a variety of subjects – or on cross-curricular themes – challenge days are run by many LEAs at weekends or in school holidays, as one-off, in-depth extension or enrichment experiences, led by specialist tutors, often from further or higher education institutions. Pupils from either KS2 or KS3 are usually nominated by their schools, usually in consultation with parents and with the pupils themselves.

Characteristics of the gifted

Gifted pupils are those who are most likely to demonstrate some or all of the abilities to do the following:

- think quickly, deeply and effectively;
- use an extensive vocabulary;
- ask penetrating questions;
- work logically and systematically;
- display remarkable powers of observation and memory;
- take on the challenge of unfamiliar tasks or new information with insight and alacrity;
- apply self with motivation, determination and concentration;
- generate creative and original solutions to problems.

Check-lists

There is a wide range of useful material to support the identification of gifted and talented children. Most schools use a balance of approaches to identification, including check-lists, such as those published by Janice Szabos, which contrasts behaviours demonstrated by bright children with those more likely to be exhibited by gifted learners, in the form of paired statements, such as 'the bright child knows the answers; the gifted learner asks the questions'. Joan Freeman sets out a check-list in the form of a series of statements under specific headings, such as 'speed of thought' and 'preference for complexity', to help teachers and parents understand the nature of high ability. Belle Wallace suggests a long list of behaviours typically exhibited by high flyers and David George suggests some early signs of giftedness. There are many other similar check-lists of criteria for identifying gifted pupils in particular, but they do not tend to be so useful when it comes to recognising pupils' talents. However, fortunately, talents are usually easier to identify by observant onlookers as they appear. (For more information about all the names mentioned here, see Who's Who.)

C

CHI

This is the acronym for the support society Children of High Intelligence (see Organisations). CHI concentrates on the top 2 per cent of the population, supporting pupils, parents and teachers and providing Saturday classes for primary-aged exceptionally able pupils.

Children as researchers

A recent initiative in Oxfordshire has been a pilot project linked both to the Westminster Institute of Education at Oxford Brookes University and to the Open University, in which primary schoolchildren – Years 5 and 6 – are taught the skills of active research. They then devise and undertake their own choice of active research projects in their schools, to be written up for publication in a professional journal and to be presented formally to an adult, university audience. They have chosen a range of topics, from children's attitudes to their parents' jobs, to whether football would be more or less popular if it was mixed, to how children watch TV. This project has already proved to be so successful that a new Children's Research Centre is planned, to be based at the Open University's campus in Milton Keynes.

Children's Palaces

After the Cultural Revolution, Children's Palaces were created all over China. Large houses and 'palaces' were used to make educational provision for children of working parents to attend after school. Nowadays children can experience a wide range of activities at these centres, including music, maths, science, puppetry, art, drama, ballet, etc. Children who wish to extend their interest in a particular area, and show motivation and commitment, are given opportunities to follow their studies to a high level. The Children's Palaces are staffed by high quality teachers and other established professionals recognised in their field. Consideration is being given to the setting up of Children's Palaces in the UK.

Children's University

This innovative project comes under the auspices of the National Primary Trust (NPT) (see Organisations). It was established to provide learning extension opportunities beyond the school day for primary school pupils, to encourage and enable them to explore subjects at greater breadth and depth and to follow their own interests and enthusiasms in their chosen directions. The Children's University's aims include the promotion of a variety of intelligences and the development of higher-order thinking skills.

CHIPS

This is an acronym for:

1   Children with High Intellectual Potential in Schools (an Australian initiative which provides additional challenge and support in schools as well as summer schools).
2   Challenging High Intellectual Potential Students in the USA (also an initiative in schools).

Cognitive ability tests (CATs)

These tests – also known as reasoning or intelligence tests – can be a very useful part of the identification and assessment procedure for gifted children. There are a variety of published tests available for all ages and most of them are very easy to administer in school, either in class, group or individual situations. There are paper-based and IT versions, assessing a range of skills associated with intelligence and reasoning. Some tests are verbal and some are non-verbal, while other tests are broken down into a number of sub-tests of specific abilities, such as spatial sequential memory or phonological awareness. Cognitive ability tests can be a valuable indicator of a child's potential – often identifying under-achieving, high-potential pupils previously unrecognised – and a useful guide to where a pupil's greatest strengths lie. Many commercial tests have the added benefit that they can generate individual pupil profiles, which can be particularly helpful to assess the relative strengths and weaknesses of a gifted child who also has learning difficulties (see Double exceptionality).

Compacting

This is a teaching strategy for highly able pupils (see Curriculum compaction).

Competitions

Each year there are many competitions for pupils in schools. Some of these are open to all children, with more able pupils extending the levels of challenge for themselves. However, there are also competitive opportunities available which are specifically designed for able, gifted or talented pupils. One example of academic challenge is the World Class Tests (see separate entry). Other types of competitive activity which might appeal are regional or national chess tournaments, debates, writing, music, poetry or sports competitions.

Concept mapping

Concept mapping was developed by Professor Joseph D. Novak in the 1960s. It is a technique for representing information in diagram form. Concept maps consist of nodes (concepts) and links (labelled lines showing the relationship between the concepts). Concept maps differ from mind maps (see Mind mapping) in that they usually have a number of nodes and a network of relationships. They can be used to communicate complex ideas, integrate old and new knowledge and organise information when problem solving.

Conceptual Challenge in Primary Schools

The Astra Zeneca Science Teaching Trust has funded this innovative project led by the Westminster Institute of Education at Oxford Brookes University, and involving Year 6 pupils in 16 Oxfordshire primary schools. A key aim is to encourage and enable teachers to improve the level of conceptual challenge for pupils in primary science.

Convergent thinking

Convergent thinking is the ability to combine a variety of facts and ideas together and evaluate them logically in order to solve a problem by identifying the single solution best suited to the given situation.

Co-ordinator for gifted and talented pupils

Co-ordinators for gifted and talented pupils are expected to fulfil a wide and varied role in schools. This may include:

- setting up agreed identification procedures of gifted and talented pupils;
- maintaining a register of gifted and talented children in consultation with teachers, parents, support staff and other professionals;
- liaising with parents, head teacher, staff, governors and LEA representatives;
- monitoring an agreed policy for identification, provision and assessment of gifted and talented pupils;
- keeping abreast of current ideas and issues related to gifted and talented education, through attending conferences, courses and reading related material;
- sharing information with school staff;
- being aware of any barriers to learning experienced by gifted and talented children and providing pastoral support;
- suggesting strategies for inclusion and differentiation;
- co-ordinating enrichment events;
- purchasing and organising resources.

The DfES Standards Site offers some guidance on the role of the gifted and talented co-ordinator. More detailed guidance can be found on the National Curriculum website (see websites). The Westminster Institute of Education at Oxford Brookes University runs the National Training Programme for Gifted and Talented Co-ordinators in the 'Excellence in Cities' initiative.

CoRT

This is a thinking skills programme devised by Edward De Bono (see Who's Who) focusing on what he calls 'attention-directing tools', to ensure that a child's attention is drawn to aspects of a situation which might otherwise be overlooked. The aim is to improve planning and decision-making. The programme comprises a variety of specific thinking 'tools', many of which encourage the child to consider all the factors and consequences of a problem or situation and to rehearse mentally all the arguments, alternatives and possible solutions (see Resources).

Creative curriculum

The Primary National Strategy (see separate entry) is leading the drive for 'Excellence and Enjoyment'. A major element is developing the creative curriculum in a variety of innovative and flexible ways, to meet more appropriately the needs of all individual pupils, especially those who are gifted or talented. Schools are being encouraged and supported to develop new and exciting ways of working, to motivate and engage children of all abilities by extending and enriching the curriculum and adapting it to their pupils' needs. Groups, networks and new projects are being set up to provide inviting and challenging opportunities between and beyond schools to develop the interests and activities of gifted and talented pupils.

C

Creative thinking

Creative thinking involves combining what is known with the active use of the imagination in order to produce new ideas and thoughts. Creative thinkers have the ability to think about a problem and solve it in an original way.

Critical thinking

Critical thinking involves the ability to analyse arguments, look for alternative ideas, see ideas from different points of view and be prepared to change your view based on reasoning and evidence.

Cross-phase links

Most cross-phase links are between primary and secondary schools, with many projects focusing on Year 6 pupils across a pyramid or federation's feeder schools. Most areas develop initiatives which enable Year 6 pupils to meet and work together. This is especially effective when it involves gifted and talented children, taking part in master classes, challenge days, sports competitions, arts or technology events. Cross-phase links which enable primary pupils to use secondary schools' facilities are also very successful, especially when activities are based in unfamiliar environments such as science laboratories, arts studios, technology rooms or sports halls, which may provide exciting new opportunities for gifted or talented pupils. In some secondary schools, collaborative activities group together Year 6 and Year 7 pupils in joint projects.

Curriculum compaction

Curriculum compaction is one way of ensuring that gifted and talented pupils do not have to cover areas of learning with which they are already familiar. Teachers need to identify a pupil's prior knowledge, skills and understanding of concepts in a subject, ensure that areas of a study unit which still need to be covered are done at the beginning of the module or term and then initiate or provide activities that will expand or enrich that subject. Compacting the curriculum means that gifted and talented pupils can work at a more challenging level and have more time for independent study. Pupils, parents and teachers need to formulate the compacted curriculum together and records need to be kept. More about curriculum compacting can be found in the work of Renzulli and Reis (see Who's Who).

D

DATT

The acronym for Direct Attention Thinking Tools, a programme developed by Edward De Bono, linked to CoRT (see CoRT).

Definitions

Definitions are useful in that they clarify identification of gifted and talented children. However, alongside this recognition we need to celebrate achievement across the whole range of activities and ability levels in order to promote endeavour, excellence and self-esteem at every level. Identification of gifted and talented children can take place most effectively when clear definitions are agreed upon and the 'labelling' of a child needs to be handled with care as it may serve to restrict rather than widen opportunities and relationships. The DfES definitions that are generally accepted are

- *Gifted* – children with high achievement or potential for high achievement in academic subjects (top 5–10 per cent).
- *Talented* – children with high achievement or potential for high achievement in sport or the creative arts (top 5–10 per cent).

Many schools continue to define children who are achieving at the upper end of the average ability range, across a number of areas of the curriculum, as *able*.

Differentiated Model of Giftedness and Talent

Francoys Gagné's Differentiated Model of Giftedness and Talent (1991) proposes a clear distinction between gifts (natural aptitudes) and talents (the systematic development of natural aptitudes to a high level through learning, training and practice). Gagné (see Who's Who) argues that a number of other factors have a tremendous impact on talent development in gifted pupils, including motivation, temperament/personality and environmental influences. If these factors are positive, the pupil will be able to develop his or her natural aptitudes to a high level.

Differentiation

Differentiation requires teachers to adapt the curriculum to meet the individual learning needs of pupils. For gifted and talented pupils we should ensure that tasks are differentiated for level, pace, complexity and depth. This may involve:

D

- allowing more independence in planning, learning and self-monitoring;
- providing open-ended tasks where learners can use a range of thinking skills and make a wider variety of connections;
- encouraging pupils to experiment, accept failure and then demonstrate task commitment by trying again using different strategies;
- providing more complex investigations and problems to solve, involving the use of metacognition;
- challenging pupils' thinking with more abstract ideas and concepts;
- providing more demanding materials and resources.

Disaffected pupils

Disaffected pupils mainly fall into three categories:

- They may start out as able under-achievers – in order either to rebel against excessive peer or parental pressure – or as an attention-seeking ploy to counterbalance lack of parental support (see Under-achievement). They may then gradually develop increasingly negative attitudes to school.

- Some gifted pupils make the deliberate choice early on to hide their high ability and under-perform in order to be accepted socially – especially by their peers – and then become depressed by the self-imposed lack of challenge.
- Others have the problem of being visual-spatial learners, which means that they tend to learn anything new as a complete concept, rather than in gradual steps, thereafter quickly becoming bored by traditional teaching methods and developing behavioural problems.

Whatever the cause, a disaffected pupil's innate giftedness may go unidentified and he or she will often become increasingly negative, withdrawn, hyperactive, aggressive or disruptive. (See Behaviour.)

Distance learning

Distance learning involves following a paper-based 'correspondence course' or an online or CD-Rom-based course, or often a combination of the two. There are a number of options, from primary/secondary modules up to Open University foundation courses (for those of most relevance to gifted and talented pupils, see Resources).

Divergent thinking

Divergent thinking is the ability to think creatively in order to find interesting and unusual solutions to open-ended problems, for which there is no single 'correct' answer. This involves looking at problems from a variety of aspects in order to generate a range of diverse and original ideas.

Double exceptionality

Double (or dual) exceptionality, also known as twice exceptionality, is the term for a child who is gifted or talented and at the same time has one or more learning difficulties or disabilities. As well as making identification more problematical, double exceptionality also constrains the opportunities and achievement of gifted children and thereby increases their frustration levels, often causing negative or disruptive behaviours, which in turn make it even more difficult to identify the child as gifted (see the work of Diane Montgomery).

Dual enrolment

Dual enrolment means that a pupil is on the roll at a mainstream school and at the same time attends another school or college – often as part of a gifted or talented acceleration programme – on a regular basis throughout the year.

E

EAZ

See Education Action Zone.

ECHA

This is the acronym for the European Council for High Ability. The main goal of the ECHA is to act as a communications network to promote the exchange of information among people interested in high ability, including educators, researchers, psychologists, parents and the highly able themselves. ECHA aims to advance the study and development of potential excellence in people of all ages (see Organisations).

Education Action Zones (EAZs)

Education Action Zones were set up by the DfES as partnerships between schools, LEAs and other local organisations and agencies, including higher education institutions and the business community. They were set up to tackle under-achievement and social exclusion in disadvantaged areas and each EAZ is run by an 'action forum'. Some EAZs focused on developing access to provision for disadvantaged gifted and talented pupils. EAZs were gradually phased out and much of their work has now been taken up through Excellence Clusters (see separate entry).

E

Emotional Intelligence

Daniel Goleman (see Who's Who) suggests that Emotional Intelligence includes five characteristics:

- self-awareness – knowing your emotions, recognising feelings as they occur, and discriminating between them;
- mood management – handling feelings so that you react appropriately to the current situation;
- self-motivation – gathering up your feelings and directing

yourself towards a goal, despite self-doubt, inertia and impulsiveness;
- empathy – recognising feelings in others and tuning in to their verbal and non-verbal cues;
- managing relationships – handling interpersonal interaction, conflict resolution and negotiations.

In his book, *Emotional Intelligence: Why It Can Matter More than IQ*, Goleman argues that these qualities are more important in our daily lives than IQ and that children should be taught these qualities.

Enrichment

Enrichment adds breadth by allowing the more able to explore 'areas of learning that other pupils do not cover, but at broadly the same level' (DfEE Excellence in Cities definition). Enrichment provides pupils with opportunities to take part in activities that have a richer and more varied content, focusing on qualitative development. Activities may take place out of the normal classroom environment.

Enrichment Triad Model

The Enrichment Triad Model was developed by Joseph Renzulli and Sally Reis (see Who's Who). It provides a comprehensive plan for enrichment that can be integrated into ordinary classrooms. The model describes three different types of enrichment activities:

- *Type 1* – these activities should provide opportunities for pupils to experience general enrichment (visits, demonstrations, performances and other activities not normally offered within the classroom).
- *Type 2* – these activities should provide opportunities for group investigation, problem solving and discussion. This is where pupils are taught how to develop their metacognitive skills.
- *Type 3* – these activities should provide opportunities for pupils to use the skills they have learned to carry out and conduct research and to find out more about an area of individual interest. Pupils select their own area of study and work independently to develop a product to share with an appropriate audience.

Eureka

This is an Israeli project, based in Jerusalem, which sets out to expose as many children as possible to opportunities in the visual arts and sciences and also offers voluntary out-of-school enrichment activities in these areas.

Excellence and Enjoyment

This document was issued to all primary schools by the DfES in autumn 2003 and it describes the main initiatives which make up the Primary National Strategy (see separate entry. See also under Creative curriculum and Thinking skills). An integral part of the Primary National Strategy – as emphasised in *Excellence and Enjoyment* – is the extension and enrichment of schools' provision for able, gifted and talented pupils. Following this initial document, the government published detailed guidelines for developing the Primary National Strategy's aims in schools, with one of its particular areas of focus being to 'develop learning skills ... the ability to think systematically ... understanding of the learning process'. The 'Understanding how learning develops' module focuses on a range of thinking skills, including creativity, reasoning, evaluation, enquiry and problem solving.

Excellence Clusters

Excellence clusters are a development of the government's Excellence in Cities programme (see separate entry). They are small groups of schools in pockets of socio-economic deprivation. Excellence Clusters have been developed in phases to work on joint projects, with the aim of developing the best possible provision (a 'distinct and discernibly different teaching and learning programme') for gifted and talented pupils in disadvantaged areas, through collaboration, support and training. Each Excellence Cluster has its own gifted and talented co-ordinator, with links to all the national organisations for gifted and talented education.

Excellence in Cities (EiC)

The gifted and talented strand of Excellence in Cities focuses on developing a range of collaborative strategies to improve the quality of differentiation at school level, to raise standards of provision for gifted and talented pupils and to pay particular attention to the ethos and attitudes towards gifted and talented pupils in all schools. A very useful evaluation of the early experience of EiC gifted and

E

talented partnerships is reported in an Ofsted document: *Providing for Gifted and Talented Pupils* (2001) (see the entry for Ofsted).

Excellence in Cities Primary Pilot and Primary Extension Project

Both of these initiatives are products of the Excellence in Cities programme (see separate entry) and focus particularly on the education of gifted and talented children in primary schools.

Excellence initiatives

Excellence initiatives are localised projects which support intensive programmes for gifted and talented students from primary and secondary schools, plus post-16 education, in more than 80 LEAs. They all build in various ways upon the Excellence in Cities model (see separate entry).

Existential intelligence

See Multiple Intelligences.

Experiential Learning

Building on previous theories about how we learn, David Kolb (see Who's Who) developed his Experiential Learning model consisting of four elements:

1. Concrete experience (carrying out a particular action).
2. Observation and reflection (seeing and understanding the effect of this action).
3. The formation of abstract concepts (understanding the general principle).
4. Testing in new situations (transferring action to a new context).

Thus Experiential Learning is a continuous cycle. Its main innovations were:

- the use of practical experience to test ideas;
- the use of feedback to change practices/ideas.

The second part of Kolb's work on Experiential Learning categorises learners as:

- *Assimilators*, who learn best when presented with sound, logical theories to consider.

- *Convergers*, who learn best when given practical applications of concepts/theories.
- *Accommodators*, who learn best when allowed to gain 'hands-on' experience.
- *Divergers*, who learn best when observing and gathering a wide range of information.

Extension

Extension means making provision for pupils to study a topic at greater depth as they 'explore areas of learning at a more demanding level than other pupils in the year group' (DfEE Excellence in Cities definition). It raises the complexity of curriculum content and involves pupils using higher order thinking and learning skills to develop a deeper understanding of a topic.

Extra-curricular activities

A range of enrichment or extension activities for higher ability children are being developed in both primary and secondary schools; many of them in non-National Curriculum subjects, such as:

- Research club
- Chess club
- Philosophy
- Latin
- Archaeology
- Algebra
- Logic
- Puzzle club
- Computers
- Ecology
- Debating.

The list of possible topics is endless, recruiting volunteers, such as members of the community, to run the more specialised activities.

Extra-mural courses/support

Extra-mural study is any externally provided course or programme (see Distance learning).

E

F

Fast-tracking

Fast-tracking is a term used to describe the moving of pupils through the education system more quickly, by taking exams early. Fast-tracking may be used for both individuals and cohorts.

G

Galilee Ecology Project

This is an Israeli initiative. The Technological Centre of Galilee invites gifted children to take part in ecology projects of the children's own devising (such as the effects of minerals on plants, or of hormones in fish). Children design and conduct investigations at the laboratories on original problems, applying to the Ministry of Education for approval and funding, taking projects through all stages to final writing and the submission of bound reports of their work and findings. This research approach is now being adopted in British schools (see Children as researchers).

GATE A

GATE A was the acronym for the Gifted and Talented Education Arm of the London Challenge, now known as 'London Gifted and Talented' (see separate entry), aimed at improving opportunities for gifted and talented students across London, including the development of a pan-London centre with a strong virtual learning community and a managed learning environment. GATE A focused on improving gifted and talented pupils' aspirations, attainment, motivation and self-esteem by providing new learning opportunities for 10–19-year-olds and by improving, extending and sharing best practice through effective collaboration between schools.

GERRIC

The Gifted Education Research, Resource and Information Centre (GERRIC) is based at the University of New South Wales in Australia. The centre is dedicated to research, training and other services in gifted education and has attained worldwide recognition for and interest in its work.

Gestalt movement

The prevailing theories of intelligence and thinking in recent years have been concerned with the 'reductionist' approach of breaking down both the process of thinking and the concept of intelligence into their constituent parts in order to gain greater understanding. The Gestalt movement, by contrast holds that considering separate elements is counter-productive, as the whole, unified totality (the 'Gestalt') of intelligence or thinking is more than the sum of its parts.

GIFT

Originally an Essex LEA service, GIFT became a separate organisation in the early 1990s and now works with gifted pupils, students and teachers in about 25 countries across the world. GIFT provides a very wide range of extension and enrichment programmes in many subjects and disciplines across England as well as abroad. GIFT delivers school-based programmes, masterclasses, day, weekend and holiday courses for primary and secondary pupils, as well as staff development services, resources, training and Inset courses. GIFT also produces teaching and learning materials for all ages (see Organisations).

Gifted

The term 'gifted' traditionally referred to outstanding performance in general intellectual ability, as measured by a standardised intelligence test. The DfES defines gifted pupils as those who have exceptional abilities in one or more subjects in the National Curriculum other than Art and Design, Music and PE (see also Talented). Recent research has presented evidence to support the broadening of these definitions (see 'Differentiated Model of Giftedness and Talent').

Governors

Schools are encouraged to appoint one of their governors to take a specific interest in the provision for gifted and talented pupils in the school and to report back to the whole governing body on a regular basis. The DfES recommends that governors' annual reports and/or school prospectuses should explain arrangements for identifying and addressing the needs of gifted and talented pupils.

G

Gregorc's Mind Styles model

This is a model of learning styles, developed by Anthony Gregorc (see Who's Who). Gregorc's Mind Styles model provides a framework for considering how the mind works. It focuses on two perceptual qualities – concrete and abstract – combined with two ordering abilities – sequential and random. All of us have aspects of each of these qualities and abilities in varying amounts. The four distinctive mind styles are:

- concrete-sequential
- concrete-random
- abstract-sequential
- abstract-random.

GTEU

This is the acronym for the DfES's Gifted and Talented Education Unit.

H

HAP

HAP is the acronym for high achieving pupil – a term often used by agencies and organisations concerned with the education of gifted and talented children. (Note that this term should not be confused with a high ability pupil.)

Headstart Programme

Headstart courses are intensive four-day residential courses that are held at major universities. They are designed for Year 12 pupils who are interested in technology-based careers. Pupils who take part in the programme usually have at least seven A or A* grades at GCSE in the relevant subjects. The course allows pupils to design, build and test projects, attend seminars and lectures and meet graduates from international organisations. They are also given the chance to find out about career opportunities in business, industry and education. Each course is monitored for quality by the Royal Academy of Engineering. The Headstart programme is actively supported by a number of major business organisations (see Organisations).

Hierarchy of human needs

In this model of his theory of motivation, Abraham Maslow (see Who's Who section) demonstrates the importance of satisfying basic needs before higher levels can be met. The hierarchy focuses on progressing from the physiological needs at the base of the pyramid-shaped model to self-actualisation and reaching one's full potential at the top. The hierarchical stages are, from the base upwards:

- sustenance – meeting physiological needs (especially food and drink);
- safety and a sense of security;
- values and being loved/loving others;
- self-esteem and being respected/respecting others;
- freedom to make choices and learn;
- appreciation and understanding of the environment;
- self-concept and self-actualisation – fulfilling one's potential.

High performance constellation

Devised by Belle Wallace (see Who's Who), this is a model of the attributes that contribute to high performance, namely:

- intelligences (see Multiple Intelligences);
- knowledge (including problem-solving and thinking skills);
- creativity (including imagination and lateral thinking);
- zeal (including motivation, sensitivity and self-esteem).

Wallace observes that high performance, reflected through these attributes, is the sum of heredity + early learning experiences + general environment.

Higher order thinking skills

Higher order thinking skills are generally considered to be those identified by Benjamin Bloom in his taxonomy. Bloom's taxonomy (see separate entry) categorises the thinking processes into various levels. The lower levels of thinking involve having a knowledge and understanding of facts while the higher levels of thinking involve analysis, synthesis and evaluation. Bloom's categories have been used by many educationists when planning teaching programmes. Teachers have been able to use Bloom's taxonomy to organise projects into challenging activities that involve the higher levels of thinking.

H

I

Identification

Identification of gifted and talented children and provision are closely linked. As challenging opportunities are made available, so children identify themselves by the response that they make to a specific learning situation. However, some gifted and talented children are not easily identified so it is advisable to use a combination of identification methods. Identification strategies will probably include:

- classroom observation
- teacher nomination
- provision
- check-lists (see separate entry)
- National Curriculum and progress assessment data
- diagnostic assessment
- Cognitive Ability Tests (CATs)
- External tests (such as end of Key Stage tests or World Class Tests)
- information from parents
- educational psychologists' assessment
- peer nomination
- self-nomination.

For identification in the early years, see Starry Night Observation Protocol.

Inclusion

The principles of inclusion require schools to provide effective learning opportunities for gifted and talented pupils, within the framework of the National Curriculum, by doing the following:

- setting suitable learning challenges (extending the breadth and depth of their study and setting challenging learning targets);
- responding to pupils' diverse learning needs (providing suitable learning environments, a variety of teaching approaches and stimulating and motivating activities);
- overcoming potential barriers to learning and assessment for individuals and groups of pupils (making provision through

the use of materials, resources and support for pupils' physical, cognitive and emotional needs).

I

Infusion method

The infusion method, devised by Swartz and Parks in 1994, focuses on the specific teaching of decision-making strategies, working through a series of relevant, thought-provoking questions which encourage thorough consideration of all angles and potential consequences, thereby enabling the child to develop his or her thinking through each step and to draw up a summarising argument or statement.

Inspection

As Ofsted Inspection Frameworks have developed and become more focused, so greater account is taken of what a school does for its gifted and talented pupils. Inspectors will be looking in particular at inclusivity: 'how far all pupils benefit, according to need, from what the school provides'. The big question throughout the inspection is 'Are the school's expectations and achievements high enough?' Inspectors will be making judgements about how well the school identifies and deals with under-achievement, challenges its most able pupils and raises standards for all.

Instrumental Enrichment

Instrumental Enrichment – a programme devised by Reuven Feuerstein (see Who's Who) – is taught outside traditional curriculum areas. He argues that those children who have difficulty in learning from experience have not been taught to structure their thinking to enable them to learn from their mistakes. He advocates 'mediated learning' in order to improve children's thinking skills. The teacher has a crucial role to play in this programme, because Feuerstein believes that it is only through systematic mediation (direct structured teaching of specific thinking skills) that children can become capable of more complex learning. The programme has 14 instruments covering activities from simple pattern detection and comparisons to complex reasoning and problem solving.

Intelligence

A clear definition of intelligence still remains a subject open to debate. In order to try to understand the nature of intelligence, we need to look at theories of intelligence.

There are two major schools of thought on the nature of intelligence. One is supported by psychologists like Eysenck, Galton, Jensen and Spearman and propounds the belief that all intelligence comes from one general factor, known as 'g'. The other believes that there are different types of intelligences. This school of thought is supported by psychologists like Gardner, Sternberg and Thurstone.

There are two arguments that support the theory of one general intelligence. Spearman (1904) found during his research that – when giving tests covering different areas of cognitive ability – there was a positive correlation, that is, some people performed well across a range of tests. Spearman called this the 'positive manifold' and referred to it as the 'g' factor. Eysenck (1982) and Jensen (1993) found that there was a correlation between neural processing speed and high IQ. They believe that neural processing speed determines the level of intelligence of an individual. These definitions of intelligence require the brain and other sensory organs to be functioning correctly.

Gardner's theory of Multiple Intelligences (see separate entry) has influenced the development of educational thinking in recent years. His theory suggests that there are a number of different forms of intelligence.

Intelligence trap

This is a phenomenon first described by Edward De Bono (see Who's Who), in which a very able thinker may approach a seemingly complex problem and immediately see a clear and logical solution, to which his or her peers happily lend their full support. The difficulty here is that the very able thinker has cut through the complexity with such apparent ease and 'jumped to the wrong conclusion' by filtering out seemingly extraneous details – some of which might have been crucial to reaching the most effective solution – without even stopping to think that his or her solution may not be the best one. Because such competent thinkers also tend to be very quick and persuasive in defending their decisions, it may be a long time before anyone realises that there might have been a better outcome. This phenomenon can often be observed in group discussions in the classroom and can be avoided through the use of a problem-solving framework (such as TASC or Thinking hats – see separate entries).

Interpersonal intelligence
See Multiple Intelligences.

Intrapersonal intelligence
See Multiple Intelligences.

IQ (intelligence quotient)
This is a measure of intelligence using a standardised intelligence test. IQ represents a person's cognitive ability at a particular point in time. IQ tests such as WISC (Weschler Intelligence Scales) and Stanford-Binet are considered to be the most reliable. The average score on an IQ test is 100. A high IQ score (above 130) indicates gift-edness but even children with low IQ scores may be gifted in areas not assessed by the IQ tests. Since 1960 most tests have been expressed as 'deviation IQs'. This means that the IQs are based on the difference between a person's score and the average score for people of the same age.

Irish Centre for Talented Youth
Based in Dublin, this is the principal centre concerned with gifted and talented education in the Republic of Ireland. Among other services, the centre runs residential and non-residential summer-school courses for 12–16 year-olds (see Organisations).

ISSP (Independent/State School Partnership scheme)
Independent State School Partnership projects have developed in various areas, with a particular focus on gaining a greater under-standing of the needs of those learners deemed to be exceptionally able. Areas of interest within ISSPs are the development of pupils' achievement through creativity, able learners as autonomous learners, KS 2/3 transition for able pupils, neurocognition and enrich-ment for able Year 6 learners.

J

Journals
Journals, or learning logs, are useful records of children's thinking and learning journeys. They are often used as part of philosophy or thinking skills work and can also help to structure and record project-based learning.

K

Key Stage 3 National Strategy

Also known as the Secondary National Strategy, this initiative aims to support schools to address the learning needs of 11–14-year-old pupils across all subjects. The Strategy is designed to be flexible to suit the context of each area and school, promoting whole-school improvement through an emphasis on teaching and learning. The Key Stage 3 National Strategy encourages high expectations and the development of personalised learning.

KWL grids

KWL stands for what a child Knows (his prior learning), what he Wants to know and what he has Learnt (at the end of the activity). A KWL grid can be used to help children organise and evaluate their learning. Children can write appropriate statements or questions under each heading to help focus their research and extend their thinking.

L

Lateral thinking

A term first devised by Edward De Bono (see Who's Who) to describe a new approach to perceptual thinking and problem-solving. Lateral thinking is about thinking in new and creative directions, away from the expected path and across conventional boundaries.

Latin

There is an increasing range of programmes for teaching and learning Latin in primary and secondary schools, in Saturday classes or independently and this subject is particularly growing in popularity among very able pupils, who appear to enjoy its logical complexity. There is also an online Latin course provided by the Cambridge School Classics Project (see separate entry and Websites).

Leading Edge Partnership

The Leading Edge Partnership programme has been designed to support groups of secondary schools – including special schools – as they work together to raise standards. This programme builds on the networks and good practice established under the Beacon school programme (see separate entry). Primary schools can become partner schools with secondary schools involved with the programme.

Leading Edge Schools

Leading Edge Schools are secondary schools which have replaced Beacon schools in sharing and disseminating good practice in specific areas, such as gifted and talented education. They are part of the Leading Edge Partnership programme (see separate entry).

Leading Practice Schools

Leading Practice Schools are primary schools which have replaced Beacon schools in sharing and disseminating good practice in specific areas, such as gifted and talented education. They are part of the Leading Edge Partnership programme (see separate entry).

L

Learnacy

Professor Guy Claxton (see Who's Who) has identified three new Rs of what he called 'Learnacy'. These are attitudes which he described as necessary elements of effective learning. Claxton's three Rs are:

- Resilience ('stickability' in uncertainty; relishing difficulty and challenge);
- Resourcefulness ('knowing what to do when you don't know what to do' – Piaget's definition of intelligence);
- Reflection (using oneself as a resource – the answer possibly lying within).

Learning styles

A learning style is the way in which we perceive, understand, organise and recall information. Researchers agree that learning styles can be distinguished, but the way that they are defined is debatable. Learning style models are based on different schools of thought. Some of the most best known are:

1. Information processing models – these refer to the way that our brains process information. They include:
    (a) the first part of Kolb's Experiential Learning Cycle, describing the processes of learning (see separate entry and Who's Who);

(b) Gardner's theory of Multiple Intelligences – referring to the way that we use our abilities to process information (see separate entry and Who's Who);

(c) Gregorc Mind Styles – showing that individuals have various combinations of strengths. These can be termed abstract-sequential, abstract-random, concrete-sequential or concrete-random (see separate entry and Who's Who).

2. Personality models – these refer to the way we interact with our environment. It is thought that our preferred learning styles are influenced by our previous learning experiences, genetic make-up, environment and culture. These models include:

(a) the second part of Kolb's Experiential Learning Cycle, describing individual learning styles;

(b) Gardner's theory of Multiple Intelligences – each individual has different abilities in up to ten areas (linguistic, logical/scientific/mathematical, musical, bodily/kinaesthetic, visual/spatial, interpersonal, intrapersonal, naturalistic, spiritual, existential);

(c) Myers Briggs Type Indicator – a revision of Carl Jung's categorisation of types of people;

(d) McCarthy's four learning styles, describing pupils as innovative learners, analytic learners, common-sense learners or dynamic learners;

(e) David George's four preferred learning styles, linked to personality types: enthusiastic, imaginative, logical and practical.

3. Perceptual Modality – this refers to the way that we take in information, using the senses. The best-known model is: VAK (Visual, Auditory, Kinaesthetic; see separate entry) – this model is used in the accelerated learning approach.

Linguistic intelligence

See Multiple Intelligences.

Loc8or

The National Academy for Gifted and Talented Youth (see Organisations) has devised the Loc8or as a talent search mechanism to locate the top gifted or talented 5 per cent of students to join the Academy. The Loc8or uses a portfolio approach. Students of all ages are asked to provide at least three pieces of evidence to support their application. Such evidence might include a teacher's letter of recommendation, examples of work or formal test results. Gifted or talented pupils are generally identified and encouraged by schools to apply to join the Academy through the Loc8or, but many others apply direct.

Logic

Many gifted or talented pupils – especially those with strengths in mathematics and/or science – enjoy challenging activities focusing on logic. Some schools offer logic as an extra-curricular activity (see separate entry), while a few incorporate logic into their classroom curriculum.

Logical-mathematical-scientific intelligence

See Multiple Intelligences.

London Challenge/London Gifted and Talented

This is a London-wide initiative for improving opportunities for pupils and the quality of education in city schools. (See GATE A, for how this initiative relates specifically to provision for gifted and talented children.)

M

Maths-by-Mail

This is an Israeli initiative, attached to the Weizmann Institute. Maths-by-Mail teaches up to 2,000 children every year, using maths challenges by correspondence, set and assessed mainly by volunteer tutors, so low-cost. (A similar science project has now been introduced.)

Masterclass

Masterclasses are usually run by guest experts, either within or between schools, and are usually for talented pupils in sports or arts subjects, such as music, art, drama, poetry, athletics, cricket or football.

Mental Literacy

The concept of Mental Literacy was originated by Tony Buzan (see Who's Who), who calls it 'the alphabet of the brain'. Mental Literacy is an understanding of how the mind works, particularly relating to memory, creativity, learning and thinking skills. Just as in literacy we use the alphabet to make words, in Mental Literacy we learn how to use the component abilities of our minds to develop our thinking and understanding. It is possible to practise all these skills and by thinking about how we improve them we also further enhance our Mental Literacy.

Mentoring

Mentors can be a great help to both the gifted/talented pupil and to the over-stretched teacher. A mentor can be a teaching assistant, a parent volunteer, a governor or a member of the community (such as a local artist or musician). Mentors can work alongside, discuss, extend thinking, challenge, encourage, motivate, inspire, assess, support or counsel gifted/talented pupils. Schools have begun to set up useful data-bases of potential mentor expertise (such as published writers, scientists, entrepreneurs or professional footballers in their communities).

Metacognition

Metacognition is the ability to reflect on our own thinking processes (thinking about the way that we think). Developing metacognitive skills can help all pupils become more independent in their learning and have a greater self-knowledge.

Mind mapping

Mind mapping is a technique developed by Tony Buzan in the late 1960s. Mind maps are similar to concept maps (see separate entry), but whereas a concept map may have several nodes (concepts), a mind map has one central concept around which a number of related ideas are written or drawn. Each of these related ideas may also have a number of related links. Mind mapping helps pupils to organise known information visually in order to understand how new knowledge is related.

MLE (Managed Learning Environment)

Through the GATE A website (see separate entry), the MLE offers an ongoing programme of live and online activities, tasks and events that provide 'challenging interactive learning'. Collaboration is encouraged between gifted and talented pupils or students across schools, boroughs, higher education institutes and other bodies. So far, this is only for those involved in the London

Challenge – of which GATE A is the gifted and talented arm – but it is hoped that this initiative will become accessible to a wider audience in future.

Monitoring

Monitoring in this context takes two forms:

- monitoring of gifted and talented children's progress and achievements;
- monitoring of overall provision for gifted and talented pupils in the school.

Monitoring of children's progress can be done through such strategies as interviews, teacher assessment, standardised test data and a range of other approaches (see Assessment).

Monitoring of school provision can be done through regular or continuous whole-school audit, through a structured self-evaluation framework, such as that devised for the Challenge Award (see separate entry), or through ongoing observation and review.

MOTIVATE

M

MOTIVATE is a unique video-conferencing project based at the University of Cambridge. It links professional mathematicians and scientists with primary and secondary schools around the world. Pupils can work on projects and problems and then present their ideas via video conferencing facilities. MOTIVATE enables pupils of all ages (5–18) – but particularly those from disadvantaged areas – to take part in live video conferences with university mathematicians and world class scientists. Pupils find out about their work and how it is used in everyday life. The MOTIVATE project started as part of the NRICH Online Maths Community in 1997 and was chosen for funding from NESTA (see Organisations) in 1999.

Motivation

Being a gifted or talented learner does not necessarily mean being a motivated learner. Similarly, a very able child may be highly motivated in areas that interest him, but very poorly motivated in areas that suit his or her parents or teachers! For a child who lacks motivation in all areas, self-esteem could well be the key to developing self-confidence and self-motivation.

Mozart Effect

The Mozart Effect is a term first used by Alfred A. Tomatis for the supposed enhancement of spatial reasoning in young children after listening to the music of Mozart. The original idea for the Mozart Effect arose from the studies of Gordon Shaw (a physicist) and Frances Rauscher (a former concert cellist and expert on cognitive development). They studied the effects of listening to Mozart on a small group of college students. Using the Stanford-Binet IQ test as a measuring tool, they found temporary enhancement of spatial-temporal reasoning in the students after listening to Mozart for ten minutes. Shaw and Rauscher created the Music Intelligence and Neural Development Institute (MIND) and have stimulated a great deal of interest and ongoing research into the effects of music on learning development, though some of this remains controversial.

Multiple Intelligences

In 1983, Howard Gardner argued against the idea that the IQ test was a complete measure of intelligence. He redefined intelligence within a new framework, as not one but several different intelligences. Gardner's theory of Multiple Intelligences initially proposed seven different intelligences, to which he has more recently added another intelligence, plus two further possibilities. These Multiple Intelligences are:

- Linguistic intelligence, characterised by strengths in working with and enjoyment of the words, meanings, structure and use of language.
- Musical intelligence involves strengths in the areas of response, sensitivity to and manipulation of sounds and rhythms.
- Logical-Mathematical-Scientific intelligence is demonstrated by strengths in the areas of mathematical and/or scientific operations, reasoning, concepts and patterns.
- Visual-Spatial intelligence comprises high degrees of visual awareness, creativity and memory.
- Bodily-Kinaesthetic intelligence is the ability to use, co-ordinate and control different parts of the body, undertaking both gross and fine motor activities in fluent, skilled and expressive ways.
- Interpersonal or social intelligence is concerned with positive relationships with others and engagement with social issues.
- Intrapersonal intelligence or intuitive intelligence is demon-

strated by insight into and control of one's self and one's own feelings, thoughts, values and attributes.

- Naturalistic intelligence encompasses the ability to recognise and classify plants, animals and minerals and to demonstrate empathy with them.

Plus possibly:

- Spiritual intelligence is concerned with cosmic issues: affective responses to the world and to the concept of a higher power.
- Existential intelligence centres on the ultimate issues of life, such as, what are we doing here?

These two last attributes are the subject of some controversy and, indeed, Gardner himself voices uncertainty regarding their status as distinct intelligences.

Gardner argues that there is a particular type of giftedness associated with each form of intelligence. Traditional teaching strategies addressed mainly a combination of linguistic and logical-mathematical-scientific intelligences, to the exclusion of all the other identified intelligences. This theory of Multiple Intelligences is a new paradigm which has ensured that the debate about intelligence has widened, becoming a much more democratic and inclusive situation than previously recognised, with considerable implications for the school curriculum. Multiple Intelligence is about appreciating pupils for who they are and the things they *can* do. Instead of asking whether a child is intelligent, we can now ask more appropriately 'In what ways is he or she intelligent?'

N

Musical intelligence

See Multiple Intelligences.

N

NACE

The National Association for Able Children in Education exists to support the daily work of teachers providing for pupils with high abilities in their classes. NACE is a large association of professionals providing a range of services, materials, training and specialist advice for teachers, LEAs, the education community, government agencies and other education professionals. Online support, a range of publications, journals and newsletters, conferences and courses are all part of NACE's provision for its members, NACE devised and administers the Challenge Award, a self-evaluation framework for schools and LEAs (see separate entry).

NAGC

The National Association for Gifted Children supports gifted and talented pupils and their parents. NAGC aims to assist children with outstanding gifts and talents to fulfil their potential and to support their parents, teachers and other relevant professionals. NAGC has a network of volunteer-run branches to provide local services for gifted and talented children. There is also a help-line, a counselling service and a youth agency for the youngsters themselves, with a magazine and website.

National Academy for Gifted and Talented Youth (NAGTY)

The National Academy for Gifted and Talented Youth (NAGTY) was established by the government in 2002. Based at the University of Warwick, NAGTY's remit is to improve educational provision for gifted and talented young people up to the age of 19 years, driving improvements in student provision by developing national leadership and support for professionals. NAGTY works in partnership with the DfES, students, parents, teachers, education professionals, specialist providers, universities and the business community. The Academy runs a range of subsidised summer schools and other outreach activities and also has a strong virtual presence.

Naturalistic intelligence

See Multiple Intelligences.

Networks

Gifted and talented co-ordinators will find it useful and supportive to join or develop networks of professionals with a specific interest in this area of education. Such networks may be national, regional or local, between schools and with other agencies. Similarly, pupils themselves can join or log onto networks of gifted and talented pupils and students, both nationally and internationally.

Nomination

Nomination is a useful element of the identification process. Self-nomination, peer-nomination, teacher-nomination or parent-nomination flags up or strengthens the possibility of a child being gifted or talented and leads to more specific assessment strategies being undertaken.

NRICH *online maths club*

The University of Cambridge offers their NRICH online maths club – a wealth of maths curriculum enrichment to support the learning of very able children of all ages, with a wide range of games, puzzles and problems, including weekly and monthly problems and themes (see Websites).

O

Ofsted findings

Ofsted have undertaken evaluations of recent initiatives in gifted and talented education, notably *Excellence in Cities and Education Action Zones: Management and Impact* (2003). Some of the main findings from this report are:

- Schools tend to select pupils who are already achieving highly and give insufficient emphasis to identifying those with potential for high achievement.
- Schools are less adept at identifying talented pupils.
- Few talented pupils in primary schools are taught by specialist teachers.
- Provision for talented pupils is fragmented and disconnected from the main work of the school, so that talents are not systematically developed.
- Strategies for the primary/secondary transfer of gifted and talented pupils are not well developed.
- The strong support of school leaders and managers for gifted and talented provision is vital for success.

This Ofsted review can be downloaded from the Archives website (see Websites).

O

Optional extension tasks

These extension tasks, for more able, gifted and talented pupils, are available on the QCA website and can be used at any time throughout the year. They are available in English, Maths and Science at

Key Stages 2 and 3 and in English and Maths at Key Stage 1.They are designed to 'motivate, engage and challenge pupils'.

P

Parallel thinking

This is a term coined by Edward De Bono (see Who's Who) to contrast with the more traditional adversarial thinking, in which solutions are arrived at from different positions through argument or formal debate. Parallel thinking happens when two or more people are co-operating in following the same or similar line(s) of thought at any one time – either together or independently – to arrive at a consensus about a solution or way forward. The direction of thinking can be changed by agreement and any contradictory thoughts or statements should be put forward for consideration – but not for argument – as the whole point with parallel thinking is to work together in 'designing' the best possible solution.

Partnerships

Partnerships and collaboration are central elements of many new initiatives in gifted and talented education. Some partnerships are part of existing initiatives, such as the London Challenge and the Leading Edge Partnership (see separate entries), while others have been set up more informally between two or more schools or between schools and higher education institutes or LEAs or other agencies/organizations. Partnerships are most effective when they have clearly defined aims and organisational frameworks.

Pathfinders

14–19 Pathfinders is a DfES initiative to test existing provision and to introduce more flexibility and choice so that students' programmes can be better tailored to their needs and aptitudes. Pathfinders therefore include initiatives focusing on gifted and talented provision.

Percentile rank

This is a term used in a number of tests that measure children's ability against a national standard. If a child is at the 50th centile in a particular test, then that means that he or she has scored the average level in that test; 50 per cent of the general school population at that age would score higher. Similarly, if a child is at the 99th centile, then only 1 per cent of the general school population would score higher. Gifted and talented children usually score in the top 5–10 per cent when compared to children of their own age.

Personalised learning

Personalised learning is an approach to teaching and learning which aims at providing optimum learning experiences for every pupil. (This differs from the more traditional concept of individualised learning, which is about providing individual learning programmes for every child.) Personalised learning focuses on designing the whole curriculum, teaching approaches and school organisation to address the needs and work towards fulfilling the potential of each individual pupil, both within and beyond the school. There are five components to personalised learning. These are:

- assessment for learning;
- teaching and learning strategies (including 'deep learning' and 'self-directed learning') and ICT strategies (incorporating new technologies);
- enabling curriculum choice and flexibility (at different depths and for different periods of time);
- organising the school for personalised learning;
- engaging with the community and beyond to develop the whole child.

Philosophy

Philosophy is increasingly incorporated into the wider curriculum in many countries as either a discrete subject or as an extra-curricular activity. Philosophy in the Classroom builds on the work of Matthew Lipman (see Who's Who) and was developed to enrich pupils' thinking skills and to stimulate discussion of their beliefs and opinions, whereby children are taught to justify their arguments with logical reasoning. They are taught to think about truth and reality across curriculum subjects and to make predictions and judgements about their changing world.

Philosophy for Children

Philosophy for Children is a specifically designed programme that involves pupils in whole class discussion on philosophical issues.

P

It introduces children and students – aged between 6 and 18 – to the idea of a community of enquiry where they can think more deeply about ideas and 'big' questions with the support of an adult facilitator. Within this community of enquiry, pupils work together to generate and answer their own questions about the philosophical issues contained in the written resources. The materials – consisting mainly of mini-novels for children and instruction manuals for teachers – aim to develop children's ability to reason from an informed point of view.

PIPAR – *Primary Innovation Project Action Research*

PIPAR involved eighteen schools nationally, was funded by the DfES and was run by Oxford Brookes University. Some of the schools involved in the project are part of the Excellence in Cities initiative and some are or were Beacon schools for their work with gifted and talented children. The aim of PIPAR is to describe models of effective practice in primary schools through case studies, which can then be used by other schools who want to develop good practice. Another aspect of the project is to support schools taking part in recognising the qualities that have led to effective provision. PIPAR also looks at the effectiveness of action research by teachers, as a tool for improving provision for gifted and talented pupils, as well as for enhancing staff development and practice.

Policies for Gifted and Talented Education

There are many useful guides to developing and writing policies for gifted and talented education in schools (see Resources). However, there are some important considerations to discuss and decide as part of the policy making process:

- definitions – of 'able', 'gifted', 'talented' and what percentage;
- identification strategies – who, how, what and when;
- approaches to classroom teaching, learning, differentiation, support;
- organisational issues – extension, enrichment, compaction, acceleration;
- opportunities – groups, days, extra-curricular, masterclasses, summer schools;
- assessment – monitoring, tracking, testing, target-setting;
- support – mentoring, guidance, counselling;

- whole-school issues – ethos, inclusion, thinking skills, climate for learning;
- roles, responsibilities and liaison – leadership, co-ordinator, parents, governor, class teacher, teaching assistants, outside professionals, specialists, organisations, higher educational institutes;
- resources – teaching, learning and reference materials, access to websites, time, personnel, training, budget;
- monitoring and review strategies as part of school self-evaluation.

Positive Cognitive Intervention (PCI)

Gifted learners need to have appropriate levels of challenge within their school curriculum if they are to work towards fulfilling their potential and not become disaffected. Positive Cognitive Intervention requires teachers to incorporate cognitive elements within their subject planning and teaching for able pupils. Such elements might include:

- encouraging reflection and creative thinking;
- think-pair-share strategies (the 'talking curriculum' linked to thinking skills);
- a range of response options, such as visual/graphic, performance, technological, oral and written, in a variety of formats;
- presenting material to be learnt as problems to be resolved;
- challenging children to think not just about what they are learning, but *how* they are learning (i.e. what strategies they are using);
- teacher comments to individuals which are both positive and constructive, linked to suggestions or questions which move the child on to a higher level;
- cognitively challenging questioning – open-ended and problem-setting questions;
- teaching philosophical approaches to extend thinking in subject learning;
- activating specific thinking skills strategies, such as the infusion method (see separate entry);
- use of brainstorming and mind mapping techniques to encourage original thinking and welcoming any unusual ideas or responses;
- simulations of subject matter to make learning more active and experiential, using problem-solving approaches;

P

- making use of a thinking skills framework, such as Bloom's tax-onomy, De Bono's thinking hats, or Wallace's TASC wheel (see separate entries).

Primary National Strategy

The Primary National Strategy unites and extends the National Literacy and Numeracy Strategies and points the way forward as described in its document *Excellence and Enjoyment* (see separate entry) and their subsequent companion guidelines to develop a creative curriculum which builds on recent successes to 'combine excellence in teaching with enjoyment in learning'. One of the ways the Primary National Strategy intends to support schools in doing this is to focus much more strongly on 'understanding how learning develops' through the explicit teaching of thinking skills. Professor Guy Claxton – who has been advising the Primary National Strategy – explains that 'the old method of what constituted good practice is very teacher-directed … it neglected young people's development as learners … The effect of this [focus on developing children's thinking about how they learn] will be that … better learners learn better.'

Prodigy

A prodigy is a child who is able to perform at adult level in a particular skill. He or she is usually of high intelligence and has well-developed metacognitive skills.

Project-Based Learning (PBL)

Project-Based Learning developed as a response to the work of John Dewey (see Who's Who), which highlighted the need for practical, relevant, pupil-centred learning activities, relating to real-life situations. This is an approach which involves the class teacher or mentor helping an exceptionally able child to initiate and structure his or her own learning through personal projects, extending and enriching his knowledge, understanding and experience. Project-Based Learning may, for example, follow on from compacting (see separate entry). PBL is often a multi-media approach, using available technologies to plan, develop, integrate and present projects. Commercial programmes are available to provide a useful framework for Project-Based Learning. Such programmes offer guidelines for subject matter, simulations of real-life situations, structure and direction, collaboration, networks and time-frames. Pupils undertaking Project-Based Learning will need to develop higher-order study, research and problem-solving skills, to integrate and evaluate their own learning and to demonstrate it to others.

Provision

The most important aspect of making provision for gifted and talented children within schools is to provide an environment that offers challenge in a supportive and enjoyable way. Gifted and talented children are first and foremost children and will thrive in a caring atmosphere where they are allowed to be themselves. It is important to provide a learning environment where children's ideas are respected and the positive value of personal endeavour and achievement is recognised. Other ways of making provision for gifted and talented pupils might include:

- enrichment activities
- summer schools
- extension activities
- extra-curricular activities
- differentiated homework
- acceleration in some curriculum areas
- fast-tracking when appropriate
- World Class Tests
- schemes of work that cater for all abilities, including the gifted and talented
- pastoral support through mentors
- links with other schools and colleges
- support from external agencies
- encouraging children to develop their metacognitive skills
- helping children to identify their learning styles
- encouraging children to set their own learning objectives.

By making effective provision for the most able children, we enhance provision for all.

Pupils-as-Teachers

This is when children either become their own teachers – devising their own learning, curricula and investigations – or when pupils help to plan the next stages of learning for the class or design computer programs or resources for class-projects.

P

Q

QADS grids

QADS stands for Questions, Answers, Details and Source(s). QUADS grids are useful aids to support children in their research work. Children write down any questions they want to find the answers to. They then write down the basic answers, the details to explain their answers and the source(s) of their information.

Questioning

Questioning can range from lower-order questioning, where pupils need to recall and understand information, to higher-order questioning that requires a greater complexity of thought and understanding. Skilful questioning, within the classroom environment, can help pupils to develop their metacognitive skills. Some questions may focus on:

- Attention (What did you notice about ...?)
- Enquiry (How can we find out about ...?)
- Comparison (How often? How long?)
- Investigation (What if ...?)
- Clarification (Can you explain why ...?)
- Philosophical (Is the glass half-full or half-empty?).

Open-ended questioning can encourage children to extend their thinking and develop a 'community of enquiry' where they can begin to both ask and answer questions together.

R

Radical Acceleration

This is an extension of the acceleration approach (see separate entry), whereby exceptionally able pupils or students are accelerated to three years or more ahead of their chronological age-group. This will be a rare occurrence and needs careful timing and educational planning, but a number of research studies have shown that, with the full support of all those involved, it can be a very successful option for the very few children who have the qualities and attributes necessary to be able to handle the various potential difficulties which may arise.

ReCAP

ReCAP is the acronym for the Research Centre for Able Pupils, based at the Westminster Institute of Education at Oxford Brookes University. It was founded in 1998 to engage in research into high ability and to provide consultancy and professional development services relating to the education of able and gifted children. ReCAP has become a major force in developing policy and practice in this field.

Rotherham Action Research (RAR)

The Rotherham Action Research programme funds early years partnership projects, linking schools.

S

Salamanca Statement

The Salamanca Statement was drawn up by the UNESCO World Conference held in Spain in 1994 and calls for inclusive education and appropriate learning opportunities to meet the needs and abilities of all children. The Statement emphasises that ordinary schools must recognise and respond to the diverse needs of all their students, so that learning must be adapted to the needs of the child, rather than the child fitted to the process.

Savant

A savant is a person who has an exceptional intuitive ability in a particular area (musical, artistic, mathematical), but has underdeveloped metacognitive skills.

SCAMPER

This is a problem-solving approach devised by Eberle, which helps children to process ideas flexibly in order to develop creative solutions. SCAMPER is an acronym for the seven stages of the process:

- Substitute
- Combine
- Adjust
- Magnify, Minify, Modify
- Put to other uses
- Eliminate, Elaborate, Enhance
- Reverse, Rearrange.

For all of these stages, the question is 'Will it improve things if I …?'

Scholarships

For talented pupils in particular, there are many specialist schools and colleges which select pupils with skills in specific subject areas, such as music, art, technology, sports, drama, dance or languages. However, there is also the possibility for a highly talented pupil of gaining a scholarship to a public school with strengths in that subject, or a specialist independent school such as a music or drama school.

Schoolwide Enrichment Model

This was developed by Renzulli (see Who's Who) and is based on the integration of two of his earlier models: the Enrichment Triad Model (see separate entry) and the Revolving Door Identification Model, which outlined procedures for the identification of pupils for various enrichment programmes.

Secondary National Strategy

See Key Stage 3 National Strategy.

Self-directed learning

This is a strategy that can be very useful for a highly able child who lacks interest or motivation in class lessons, probably covering subject content he or she already knows well but that the rest of the class needs to revise or practise. Self-directed learning usually involves gifted pupils devising and undertaking their own choice of project or research, or possibly practical assignments. However, it may be that the teacher or a mentor directs the choice of topic to provide continuity with the learning of the rest of the class, but still enables the pupil to direct his or her own learning within that subject area. It may be very useful for the pupil to use mind maps or for the class teacher or mentor to provide a thinking skills framework (such as Bloom's taxonomy or the TASC wheel – see separate entries) to encourage and organise purposeful learning, whatever the context. (See also Project-Based Learning.)

Self-esteem

Self-esteem means the way that we evaluate ourselves as individuals. Gifted and talented pupils with high self-esteem are convinced of their own abilities, have a positive attitude, feel in control of their lives and their learning and have a strong feeling of self-worth. Gifted and talented pupils with low self-esteem often feel different, have a poor opinion of their ability, have a negative attitude to life and learning and compare themselves unfavourably to their peer group.

Self-Evaluation Framework (Challenge Award)

This Challenge Award Self-Evaluation Framework was devised by NACE (see separate entry) to provide a standard by which schools can evaluate and plan for continuous whole-school development of their gifted and talented provision. It consists of ten elements, which together represent good quality provision. Each element contains objective criteria and suggested evidence of what to look for when auditing practice. The Self-Evaluation Framework is a central part of working towards the Challenge Award, which recognises and celebrates high quality gifted and talented provision. It can also be used independently to monitor and develop provision in any school. (See Challenge Award.)

Self-nomination

Self-nomination is when a gifted or talented child identifies himself or herself as having his or her gift/talent(s) and may also suggest strategies for his or her own development. In school, this strategy may seem superfluous in some cases, but many highly able children develop out-of-school hobbies or interests, often to a high level, which may be unknown to their teachers. It is very helpful for a school to know about a child's passion for astro-physics, ancient history, sculpture or electronics, for example, and this may well signal for the first time that an otherwise quietly studious or under-achieving pupil may be gifted or talented. Similarly, if schools are able to introduce unusual subjects as extra-curricular activities (see some suggestions under separate entry) or encourage individual research projects within school on topics of interest, a child with low self-esteem may well have his or her confidence boosted and new interests awakened to be further pursued in his or her own time.

SNAP

The acronym for the Scottish Network for Able Pupils (see Organisations).

Somerset Thinking Skills

The Somerset Thinking Skills programme is based on Feuerstein's Instrumental Enrichment Programme. It uses the same basic principles of mediation, bridging and transfer, but the materials are pictorial and naturalistic, relating to familiar settings and experiences. Somerset Thinking Skills is a structured, cumulative and sequential programme that can be taught in a multi-sensory way. The programme is arranged in seven modules, each of which focuses on a specific aspect of learning and problem solving. A handbook provides details of the aims and objectives of the course as well as explaining the underlying theoretical principles (see Resources).

Spiritual intelligence

See Multiple intelligences.

Sports approach

Professor Joan Freeman (see Who's Who) suggests that a range of facilities should be made available to pupils out of school hours, in the same way that sports facilities are made available to those who are talented and motivated in sports. Freeman believes that all youngsters should be given opportunities to select themselves to focus on any subject at a more advanced and broader level. The sports approach involves pupils in educational decision-making and teachers in identifying gifted and talented children by provision.

Starry Night Observation Protocol

This is an identification procedure, developed in Nebraska and based on observations of children's behaviour, which can help to identify potential in young children in a non-cultural and non-traditional way. The Starry Night Observation Protocol (see also Young, gifted and talented) identifies a range of behaviours which help to give teachers a better understanding of the children's potential through observing their behaviour, aptitude and learning preferences. It was adapted for use in English Schools in 1993 and was updated in 2004, to suit the Foundation Stage, by Johanna Raffan (see Who's Who), working with schools in Dorset, as a useful and practical observational identification procedure. A description of the Starry Night Observation Protocol can be found in Deborah Eyre's book *Able Children in Ordinary Schools*, pp. 30–33 (see Resources).

Summer schools

The national summer schools programme for gifted and talented 10–14-year-olds has been running since 1999 and now runs in all English LEAs. Summer schools provide for gifted pupils (those with academic ability), talented pupils (those with ability in art, music, sport and other areas of the creative arts) and those who are 'all-rounders' (with high ability in both gifted and talented areas). Staff in nominating schools are expected to use both quantitative data and qualitative information when identifying pupils for attendance. Summer schools usually provide for Years 6–9 pupils, but some extend this to Years 10 and 11. The government funds at least half of all summer school places to be made available to Year 6 pupils, so there is a strong emphasis on primary/secondary transition. There are more than 500 summer schools every year, each catering for at least 30 pupils, drawn from the most able 5–10 per cent of pupils from each participating school. Summer schools generally provide 50 hours of contact time, usually over a ten day period in the school summer holidays. NAGTY also provides an extensive programme of summer schools (see separate entry).

T

Talented

The Department for Education and Skills defines talented pupils as those who have exceptional abilities in Art and Design, Music, Sport or the Performing Arts. Recent research has presented evidence to support the broadening of these definitions (see Differentiated Model of Giftedness and Talent).

Tall poppies

Tall poppies are those which grow tall and stand out above the field. Some farmers cut them down; others nurture them. In both New Zealand and Australia, this term has been adopted to refer to gifted and talented children. Tall Poppies Learning Centres are partially funded by the New Zealand government to provide a choice of activities based on high-interest topics to suit many different abilities and learning styles, including high levels of challenge and independence.

TASC

The TASC framework (Thinking Actively in a Social Context) was devised by Belle Wallace (see Who's Who) as an outcome of international research into problem-solving programmes. The TASC wheel is a framework for clarifying and developing learners' thinking and learning skills. It incorporates logical, creative and evaluative thinking processes in a structured series of strategies:

- gather and organise – making links with prior learning and bridging to new learning;
- identify – understanding and communicating the task and desirable outcomes;
- generate – generating ideas, researching knowledge;
- decide – the best way to approach the task;
- implement – address the task using appropriate intelligences;
- evaluate – reviewing how desirable outcomes have been met;
- communicate – sharing work with an audience;
- learn from experience – the metacognitive stage, reflecting on own learning.

Taxonomy

A taxonomy is a classification system or framework, such as Bloom's taxonomy (see separate entry).

Teacher's Bistro

The Teacher's Bistro is a website service for teachers of gifted and talented students, provided by the National Association for Gifted Children (see Organisations and Websites). It focuses on synthesising research and ideas for middle and secondary school teachers and includes a range of topics, support and links.

TEEP

This is an Australian project. TEEP stands for the TalentEd Enrichment Programme, which provides Internet-based courses for gifted children, encouraging self-directed investigation and problem-solving.

Thinking Hats

This model, developed by Edward De Bono (see Who's Who), provides a scaffold for thinking about a problem or an issue. There are six hats, each representing a different aspect of the thinking process:

- Blue Hat – process (reflecting on thinking);
- Red Hat – feelings (emotions, senses and intuition);
- Green Hat – creativity (considering new possibilities and creative alternatives);
- Yellow Hat – optimism (considering the advantages and benefits);
- Black Hat – caution (considering disadvantages, negatives, risks, costs);
- White Hat – information (considering facts and questions to ask).

Thinking Hats can be used separately or together – by all age-groups – to consider problems and create solutions.

Thinking skills

Thinking skills are the mental processes through which we acquire, interpret, store, retrieve, reorganise, analyse, synthesise, evaluate and reflect on knowledge. Carol McGuinness, in her review *From Thinking Skills to Thinking Classrooms* identifies three approaches to the teaching of thinking skills:

1. Structured thinking skills programmes, favouring a generalist approach but not linked to a particular area of the curriculum.
2. Subject specific programmes, focusing on developing high level thinking within a particular subject area.
3. Infusion methodology – this approach identifies contexts where particular thinking skills and strategies can be developed and used across different areas of the curriculum. Thinking needs to be explicitly discussed. (See Infusion method.)

The National Curriculum Handbook states: 'By using thinking skills pupils can focus on "knowing how" as well as "knowing what" – learning how to learn.' The thinking skills listed below are meant to complement the key skills and are embedded in the National Curriculum:

- information-processing skills;
- reasoning skills;
- enquiry skills;
- creative thinking skills;
- evaluation skills.

The Primary National Strategy has embarked – through its 'Excellence and Enjoyment' initiative – on providing guidelines for schools to teach a range of thinking skills in order to develop in their pupils a better 'understanding of how learning develops'. These DfES guidelines are being disseminated to all primary schools in *Excellence and Enjoyment: Learning and Teaching in the Primary Years* (2004). Some of the thinking skills to be explicitly taught include creativity, reasoning, evaluation, enquiry and problem-solving. (See Primary National Strategy and Excellence and Enjoyment.)

Thinking through Geography

Thinking through Geography is a programme designed by David Leat and his team at the University of Newcastle in partnership with geography teachers. A list of concepts, necessary to the understanding of geography, has been identified. Twenty-four lessons have been developed, each of which target a concept. The lessons encourage the children to talk about their own thinking, help them to develop their vocabulary and evaluate alternative solutions to problems.

Three Ring Conception of Giftedness

Renzulli (1986) (see Who's Who) constructed this model to show the three interdependent characteristics that he believed were essential to the concept of giftedness. They were:

- above average ability;
- creativity;
- task commitment.

Tomorrow's Achievers

This is an initiative to provide masterclasses for exceptionally able children and young people (see Organisations).

Tortoise Mind

The concept of a slow mind potentially leading to more intelligent outcome was developed by Professor Guy Claxton in his book *Hare Brain, Tortoise Mind* (see Resources). His proposition is that there is a part of the brain which will subconsciously mull over a problem, in a reflective way, while we carry on with ordinary events of daily life. This part of the brain needs time off task and away from the problem itself to digest and process all the available information and work in the background – as it were – to make connections and generate potential solutions. Claxton hypothesised that – instead of trying to race to achieve immediate solutions – if we allow this type of subliminal reflection to develop, we are increasing the power of our intelligence.

Transfer/transition

A recent Ofsted report (see Ofsted findings) of provision for gifted and talented pupils in schools found that: 'Strategies for the primary/secondary transfer of gifted and talented pupils are not well developed.' Schools are developing increasingly focused, collaborative transition projects for their pupils. The most effective transition projects between two or more schools – usually primary/secondary – focus on specific subjects or themes and have clear aims and time-scales. It is crucial that all appropriate information is passed on from primary to secondary schools regarding gifted and talented pupils' abilities, experiences, achievements and needs. Both National Strategies include a focus on improving strategies for transfer between Key Stages.

Triarchic theory

Sternberg's (see Who's Who) triarchic theory of intelligence comprises three elements of our thinking processes:

- componential (analytical or logical) thinking focuses on planning, monitoring, reflection and transfer;
- experiential (creative or problem-solving) thinking focuses on developing and applying new ideas and creating solutions;
- contextual (practical) thinking focuses on selecting and shaping real-world environments and experiences.

Sternberg recognised that people are likely to have a combination of any two or all three of these elements and that how well this would equip them to succeed would rely on interactions between these elements, the chosen activity and other aspects of an individual's profile, such as personality and culture.

Triune Brain

Paul MacLean (see Who's Who) developed the Triune Brain theory, in which he claimed that the brain is actually three brain-systems in one:

- *The reptilian system* (relating to physical survival and mainte-
  nance). The importance of the reptilian system to learning is
  that if a learner feels anxious, stressed or fearful, the 'fight or
  flight' response takes over and effective learning is no longer
  possible. The reptilian complex is highly resistant to change.
- *The limbic system* (controlling sensory information, emotions
  and long-term memory). This system is strongly involved in
  experiential and information-gathering learning processes, con-
  verting learning into memory.
- *The neocortex* (controls higher-order cognitive processes, language and problem-solving). This system makes up the largest
  part of the human brain and links closely with the limbic system
  to coordinate thinking, emotion, memory and voluntary action.

These systems are three layers of the brain, which interconnect and
interact in day-to-day activities and thought-processes.

Twice exceptionality

This is another name for Double exceptionality (see separate entry).

U

Under-achievement

Able under-achievers may be failing to achieve their potential in
school for a number of reasons: some of them within the child's
control and others for external reasons. For example, for some children it might be a coping or rebelling behaviour, to evade undue
attention, taking the view that it's easier to fade into the background than to strive to fulfil high expectations. For other children
it may be a way of gaining acceptance from their less gifted peers.
Under-achievers may exhibit any of the following behaviours:

- coasting;
- orally very good but written work poor/incomplete/lacks
  lustre;
- apparently bored, lethargic and unmotivated;
- restless and inattentive;
- not interested in gaining the teacher's approval;
- in a world of their own;
- impatient, critical and sometimes impudent;

- lacking perseverance and reluctant to do routine work;
- emotionally unsettled, frustrated and having low self-esteem;
- self-sufficient, careless and indifferent;
- setting inappropriate goals (too low or too high);
- playing the 'class clown' and distracting others.

At the same time, able under-achievers may exhibit some of the positive traits of giftedness (see Characteristics of the gifted). However, many very able under-achievers mask their abilities so well that they may remain unidentified and therefore insufficiently challenged in school, often resulting in disaffection and behavioural difficulties (see separate entries).

V

VAK learning styles

It is claimed that we each have a dominant learning style, often called a 'preferred learning style', and that if we are given more opportunities to use our dominant style we tend to learn in a more natural way, making learning easier. VAK (Visual, Auditory, Kinaesthetic) are ways in which we give and receive information. Visual learners understand new concepts more readily when they are presented in a written, pictorial or diagrammatic format. Auditory learners understand new concepts more easily when they are explained and discussed within the class. Kinaesthetic learners understand new concepts more easily when they are presented through a practical, hands-on approach, allowing pupils to move around and to use concrete materials.

Virtual School for the Gifted (VSG)

The Virtual School for the Gifted is an Australia-based online school, with students in many countries. The VSG provides a range of online courses to challenge able students of all ages. It works with schools and homes and specialises in providing enrichment courses to complement and extend the regular curriculum, to provide intellectual challenge and to give able students an online community with their own discussion groups (see Websites).

Visual-spatial intelligence

See Multiple Intelligences.

W

World Council for Gifted and Talented Children (WCGTC)

The World Council for Gifted and Talented Children has its head-quarters in California, USA. The WCGTC is a global network of educators, scholars, researchers, parents, educational institutions and others interested in giftedness. Biennual World conferences are held in different locations and are attended by elected delegates from a long list of member countries. The UK delegates to the WCGTC from 2003 to 2005 are Deborah Eyre (of NAGTY), Tony Hurlin and Johanna Raffan (of NACE).

World Class Arena

World Class Arena is an international initiative set up initially by the DfES and designed to identify and assess students around the world. At the heart of the World Class Arena are World Class Tests (see separate entry). It also offers classroom support materials and resources.

World Class Tests

World Class Tests in maths and problem-solving (in maths, science and design technology) are aimed at identifying and challenging able pupils aged 8–10 and 12–14, but this suggested age-range is flexible. They are part of a global programme known as the World Class Arena (see separate entry). The tests themselves are partly paper-based and partly on the computer. Each test requires pupils to apply creative thinking and logic, by demonstrating their ability to process and respond to unfamiliar information and communicate their thought processes coherently. World Class Tests are available all over the world and have been taken in many countries, including Australia, New Zealand, Hong Kong, Saudi Arabia, Slovenia, the United Arab Emirates, Canada, the United States and the United Kingdom. They are available in English and there is also a Chinese version. (See Websites.)

X

Xcalibre

This is a website directory of resources for teachers of gifted and talented pupils, intended to complement National Curriculum guidance. It is gradually extending its services to teachers and is intended to become a major portal for gifted and talented education, linking all relevant websites. (See Websites.)

Y

Young gifted and talented

Research by Joan Freeman shows that some gifted and talented children can be identified very early in their lives. These children may appear outstanding in particular areas of their development, such as their use of language, social interaction, manipulation of numbers, conceptual understanding or artistic ability. However, some young gifted and talented children may not be so easily identified, particularly those who are working in a different language or those who have learning difficulties (see Double exceptionality). The Starry Night Observation Protocol (see separate entry) can provide a useful framework for the identification of young children's gifts and talents.

Y

Youth Agency

A service of the National Association for Gifted Children (see separate entry and Organisations), the Youth Agency is a network of young people, aged 11–20 who have exceptional gifts and talents.

Youth Café

The Youth Café is a website for gifted and talented 11–20-year-olds, funded by the Youth Agency (see separate entry) and included in the British NAGC's website. It includes interactive sections, advice, subject links and various resources, including events, contests and clubs.

Youth Sport Trust Project

The Youth Sport Trust has drawn up a national framework for the development of gifted and talented sports students, from 18 months to 18 years of age (see Organisations).

Z

Zone of proximal development

Lev Vygotsky (see Who's Who) introduced the term 'zone of proximal development' to describe the difference between what a child can achieve on his or her own when solving problems and his or her potential for achievement when given the optimum support from his or her teachers and peers. 'Scaffolding' is often used to describe how teachers and able peers can help children move on to the next stage of their development, by modelling a skill or explaining a concept. By explaining what they are doing and why, they are giving pupils opportunities to practise and internalise that skill.

Who's Who

B

Binet, Alfred

In 1904 Alfred Binet, a French physician, was asked to develop a way of differentiating between those students who were educable and those who were uneducable. He developed a test that required the individual to understand complex ideas across a range of processes of the mind. The test determined a child's mental age and was the forerunner of IQ tests. Binet did not believe that a person's intelligence was fixed and felt that the tests would help him to provide appropriate teaching for those children identified as mentally backward.

Bloom, Benjamin

In 1956 Benjamin Bloom led a group of educational psychologists who developed a six-level classification for intellectual development. Bloom found that over 90 per cent of test questions encountered by pupils required them to use the lowest order of thinking (recall of information). According to Bloom's taxonomy: knowledge, comprehension and application required lower levels of thinking while analysis, synthesis and evaluation required more complex, higher levels of thinking. (See Bloom's taxonomy.)

Borkowski, John G.

Dr John Borkowski is Professor of memory, cognitive development and intelligence in children at Notre Dame University, Indiana, USA. He is known particularly for his work on metacognition and its importance as a component of intelligence. His 'signs of intelligence' model shows how inherited factors influence the development of environmentally learned thinking and problem-solving skills.

Bruner, Jerome Seymour

Jerome Bruner is an American psychologist, best known for his work in cognitive psychology, particularly the development of language and communication. Like Vygotsky, Bruner emphasised the need to 'scaffold' children's learning by providing structure. He advocated a system of teaching where the content of a topic was gradually developed and extended over a period of time with each lesson building on previous work covered. He called this 'the spiral curriculum'. Bruner's research also emphasised the importance of the need to focus on key concepts and revisit them at higher levels with the help of adult 'scaffolding'.

Buzan, Tony

Tony Buzan is the President of the Brain Foundation, Founder of the Brain Trust, international trainer and author of many best-selling books on the brain and learning. He also acts as a coach for the British Olympic Chess Squad. He lectures throughout the world and acts as a consultant and adviser to a number of organisations. He is the originator of Mind maps, Lateral thinking and the concept of Mental literacy (see separate entries).

C

Cattell, Raymond B.

Dr Raymond Cattell was an English psychologist who proposed the theory that general intelligence comprises two principal independent abilities. He called these 'Fluid Intelligence', which encompasses reasoning and problem-solving, and 'Crystallised Intelligence', which is the assimilation and application of cultural knowledge.

Clark, Barbara

Dr Barbara Clark is a Professor at California State University, Los Angeles, where she co-ordinates graduate programmes in gifted education. She is also trustee and director of the Center for Educational Excellence for Gifted and Highly Able Learners, Past President of the California Association for Gifted Children and was formerly a US delegate and Past President of the World Council for Gifted and Talented Children. Her 'Integrative Education Model' demonstrates how research into how the mind works can provide a basis for optimising teaching and learning, by linking thinking, feeling, intuition and physical sensitivity in mutually supportive ways to develop the potential of gifted children.

Claxton, Guy

Professor Guy Claxton is Visiting Professor of Psychology at the University of Bristol and an international speaker and writer who has a particular interest in the science of learning and the part that subconscious thinking, ambiguity and paradox can play in the development of intelligence. His acclaimed book *Hare Brain, Tortoise Mind* (see Resources) considers research findings in this area of learning and intelligence (see also Tortoise mind). Claxton also identified the new 'three Rs' of Learnacy (see separate entry), which he explained in his book *Wise Up*.

D

De Bono, Edward

Edward De Bono is a leading international speaker and world authority on creative thinking. He is the originator of the terms 'lateral thinking' and the 'intelligence trap' (see separate entries). De Bono developed a variety of widely used programmes for developing thinking skills, of which the best known are DATT (Direct Attention Thinking Tools), the CoRT thinking programme – arising out of De Bono's Cognitive Research Trust – and his Six Thinking Hats, which have been adapted for use worldwide by all ages and in all situations and settings (see Resources).

Dennison, Paul E.

Paul Dennison is an educational therapist who devised Educational Kinesiology, popularly known as 'Brain Gym' (see separate entry). This is the science of body movement and the relationship of muscle and posture to brain function and is particularly relevant to the development of thinking skills and emotional intelligence through 'Accelerated learning'. Dennison discovered that cross-crawl activity worked by stimulating both hemispheres of the brain. This finding has subsequently been applied to a range of activities planned to use both sides of the body in order to maximise brain functions in developing thinking skills.

Descartes, René

René Descartes was a French mathematician, scientist and philosopher. He lived at a time when traditional ideas were being questioned and he wanted to devise a method for reaching the truth. He coined the Latin phrase 'cogito ergo sum' ('I think, therefore I am'). His method of systematic doubt had a tremendous impact on the development of philosophical thinking.

Dewey, John

John Dewey was an American psychologist, philosopher and educator who emphasised the importance of practical ideas in both his philosophical and educational theories. His ideas prompted a change in education in the USA in the first half of the twentieth century. Dewey's philosophy was about dealing with problems that arose out of real situations. He therefore opposed didactic teaching methods and advocated practical learning experiences. From this approach developed Project-Based Learning (PBL) (see separate entry).

E

Eyre, Deborah

One of the foremost contributors to the field of Gifted and Talented education in the UK in recent years. Professor Deborah Eyre is the Director of the National Academy for Gifted and Talented Youth, based at Warwick University. She has been an adviser on gifted education to both the government and a wide range of LEAs. She is a UK Delegate of the World Council for Gifted and Talented Children and, prior to taking up her post at the National Academy, she was Deputy Head of the Westminster Institute of Education at Oxford Brookes University and Director of ReCAP, its Research Centre for Able Pupils. She was also President of NACE between 1997 and 1999. Deborah Eyre has written a number of seminal works on the subject of gifted and talented education, one of the best-known being *Able Children in Ordinary Schools*.

F

Feuerstein, Reuven

Rumanian-born, Reuven Feuerstein was a student of Carl Jung and Jean Piaget. His programme of intervention, Instrumental Enrichment (see separate entry), is founded on the belief that intelligence is not a fixed quality, determined at birth, but that it is variable and can be developed at every stage of life. Feuerstein is considered to be one of the twentieth-century's leading psychologists, whose methods are recognised as being effective in schools and a variety of other settings worldwide. At his International Center for the Enhancement of Learning Potential, Feuerstein works with children considered to be uneducable, including a number of Down's Syndrome children. Feuerstein's work shows that, if barriers to learning are identified, and if children are given opportunities to learn, using their strengths through mediated learning experiences, the quality of their education is enriched and they are more able to reach their potential.

Fisher, Robert

Robert Fisher runs the Centre for Research in Teaching Thinking at Brunel University. He is a key speaker at both national and international conferences on teaching thinking and Philosophy for Children. He has written a number of books on problem solving, teaching thinking and philosophy (see Resources).

Freeman, Joan

Professor Joan Freeman is a psychologist who has written many books and articles related to her studies of gifted and talented children. She began her detailed longitudinal study of 210 children in 1974, comparing the recognised gifted and the unrecognised gifted with their peer group. From this study she wrote three books following their development. She has also written two major reports for the UK government and has acted as a consultant to many gifted and talented organisations around the world. She is Visiting Professor at Middlesex University, London, and Founding President of the European Council for High Ability (ECHA), and a Patron of NACE.

G

Gagné, Francoys

Professor Francoys Gagné is best known for his Differentiated Model of Giftedness and Talent (see separate entry), for which he won a MENSA award in 1998. This model proposes a clear distinction between gifts (natural aptitudes) and talents (systematic development of natural aptitudes to a high level). Professor Gagné also won an American MENSA award in 1993 for his research on gender differences in high abilities. His research interests include:

- the study of people with multiple talents;
- the role of aptitudes in theories about talent fostering in education, arts and sports;
- the interaction between aptitudes, interests, personality and environmental factors in the choice of a talent area and in progress in that talent field.

Gardner, Howard

Howard Gardner is Professor of Education at Harvard Graduate School of Education, Professor of Neurology at Boston University School of Medicine and Co-Director of Harvard Project Zero – a long-term study of human intellectual and creative development. He has written a number of books and many articles relating to his research in the area of cognitive science. He is best known for his theory of Multiple Intelligences (see separate entry). In this theory he challenged the idea that there existed only one human intelligence, that could be assessed using standard psychometric tests. In his book, *Frames of Mind: The Theory of Multiple Intelligences*, Gardner proposed a range of different intelligences to account for the broad range of human potential. In another book, *Extraordinary Minds*, Gardner identifies three specific features which he associates with extraordinary achievements:

- leveraging – the ability to ignore one's weaknesses and exploit one's strengths;
- reflection – in order to come to know one's strengths and weaknesses;
- framing – the ability to construe one's experiences in a positive way.

George, David

Dr David George has taught in a range of educational settings. He was the Founder President of NACE and has written and lectured both nationally and internationally on the education of gifted and talented children. He was an Executive Member of the World Council for Gifted and Talented Children and a consultant to the British Council and to UNESCO.

Goleman, Daniel

Dr Goleman was co-founder of the Collaborative for Academic, Social and Emotional Learning, which aimed to help schools introduce emotional literacy courses. He consults and lectures internationally on Emotional Intelligence (see separate entry). In his book, *Emotional Intelligence: Why It Can Matter More than IQ*, he argues that qualities such as self-awareness, self-discipline, persistence and empathy are more important in our daily lives than IQ and that children should be taught these qualities.

Gregorc, Anthony F.

Formerly a high school teacher and now attached to the Universities of Illinois and Connecticut in the USA, Dr Anthony Gregorc is best known for his pioneering work in teaching and learning styles, especially his Mind Styles Model (see separate entry).

H

Horn, John

A prominent US researcher in the field of intelligence, John Horn further developed Cattell's theory of fluid and crystallised abilities and suggested that crystallised ability increases with age, whereas fluid ability increases in the early years, plateaus and then decreases.

J

Jensen, Eric

Eric Jensen is the author of many books on brain-based learning. He is the co-founder of SuperCamp, The Brain Store and Jensen

Learning Corporation. He is a member of the Society for Neuroscience and the New York Academy of Science and is a popular speaker at many conferences.

K

Kolb, David A.

Dr David Kolb is Professor of Organisational Behavior at the Weatheread School of Management in the USA. He is best known for his work on Experiential Learning (see separate entry), including learning styles.

Koshy, Valsa

Valsa Koshy is co-director of the Brunel Able Children's Education Centre (BACE) at Brunel University, Britain's first university-based research and teacher-support centre for gifted children. BACE has links with international centres in the USA and Australia. Valsa Koshy has written or edited a number of books on teaching able and exceptionally able children and devised, with her BACE co-director, Ron Casey, the 'Special Abilities Scales' for identifying and assessing high potential pupils (see Resources).

L

Leat, David

David Leat is Reader in Curriculum Innovation at the University of Newcastle. He and his team developed 'Thinking through Geography' (see separate entry), in partnership with geography teachers at the Thinking Skills Research Centre at Newcastle University. Leat was seconded as a national consultant for the Department of Education and Skills Key Stage 3 Strategy and has published work on the teacher's role in developing pupils' metacognition.

Lipman, Matthew

Matthew Lipman is Director of the Institute for the Advancement of Philosophy for Children and Director of the Institute for Critical Thinking, Montclair State University, USA. He developed 'Philosophy for Children' (see separate entry) with Ann Margaret Sharp in the 1970s. Since then both he and his colleagues have continued to develop materials for use in schools with children from 6 years old, to help them develop as thinkers. Lipman believes that children are natural philosophers and that teachers need to encourage children's curiosity and questioning as a starting point for philosophical enquiry.

Lozanov, Georgi

In the 1970s, Georgi Lozanov introduced a technique called 'Suggestopedia' into his classroom. This technique introduced the idea of positive suggestion into the way that young people learn, while at the same time eliminating negative suggestion. Lozanov used music and colour during his teaching sessions, believing that they helped to fix key points into the learner's subconscious mind. He also emphasised the importance of developing a clear framework for each teaching session. It was some years before Lozanov's original ideas were incorporated within a range of techniques now known broadly by the term 'accelerated learning' (see separate entry).

M

MacLean, Paul

Dr Paul MacLean, the neurologist and former director of the Laboratory of the Brain and Behavior in the United States Institute of Mental Health, developed the theory of the Triune Brain, incorporating:

- the reptilian complex – controlling physical and survival functions;
- the limbic system – controlling sensory information and memory;
- the neocortex – controlling higher-order cognitive processes.

MacLean suggests that these three layers of the brain interlink and interact to coordinate memory, emotion, thinking and action.

Maslow, Abraham

Abraham Maslow was a psychologist who wrote extensively on the subject of mental health and human potential. He became the

M

leader of the humanistic school of psychology that emerged in the 1950s and 1960s. Maslow is best known for his theory of motivation, the 'Hierarchy of human needs' (see separate entry). Based on years of research and observations, Maslow proposed that human beings had to satisfy their most basic needs before they could move up the hierarchy and reach their full potential as individuals.

McGuinness, Carol

Dr Carol McGuinness is Professor of Psychology at Queen's University, Belfast. She is the author of numerous publications on thinking skills and produced a report for the DfES entitled *From Thinking Skills to Thinking Classroom* (1999). She directed the ACTS project (see separate entry) in Northern Ireland, which developed and evaluated methodology for enhancing children's thinking skills across the curriculum.

Montgomery, Diane

Professor Diane Montgomery, a former science teacher and chartered psychologist, is the leading expert in the field of Double exceptionality (see separate entry). She is Professor Emeritus at Middlesex University and a Patron of NACE. Professor Montgomery is the Director of the Learning Difficulties Research Project in Maldon and leads a number of programmes related to both SEN and gifted and talented education. She is the author of a number of seminal books and articles on the subject of double exceptionality and is the Editor-in-Chief of the NACE journal *Educating Able Children*.

P

Perkins, David

Dr David Perkins was a founder-member and Co-director of 'Project Zero' at Harvard, which focuses on the psychology and philosophy of education in the arts, including particularly cognitive development and skills. He has undertaken a lot of work on the interlocking relationships between thinking, learning and understanding, which depend on thinking about one's learning. He emphasises that learning can be considerably improved by explicit teaching for transfer, focusing on higher-order cognitive skills and the use of Project-Based Learning (see separate entry). Perkins suggests that IQ has three major dimensions:

- neural intelligence – the efficiency and precision of the neuro-logical system;
- experiential intelligence – based on accumulating knowledge and experience;
- reflective intelligence – the system that controls neural and experiential intelligence.

There is general agreement that neural intelligence has a 'use it or lose it' characteristic, and that it can be both maintained and increased through usage. Reflective intelligence can be improved and strengthened through metacognitive approaches to learning.

Piaget, Jean

Jean Piaget, a Swiss psychologist, was well known for his work in the field of child development and learning. Piaget was fascinated with the reasoning that children used to answer questions. His theories were based on the idea that, as children develop, they build cognitive structures or concept networks to help them understand and respond to physical experiences within their environment. Piaget identified four developmental stages through which most children progress:

1. Sensory-motor – birth to 2 years – when children interact with objects but are not aware that they remain in existence when they are out of sight.
2. Pre-operational – 2 to 6 years – when children need to experience concrete, physical situations.
3. Concrete-operational – 7 to 11 years – when children can begin to experience abstract problems.
4. Formal-operational – 11 to 15 years – when children begin to develop conceptual reasoning.

Piaget argued that children's cognitive structures become more sophisticated as they move through each stage of development.

R

Raffan, Johanna

Johanna Raffan, formerly a primary school headteacher, has developed her expertise in the field of gifted and talented education throughout her career and is now one of the foremost advisers in the UK, working with the government, groups of schools, LEAs and regions, such as Dorset and Wales, on a range of initiatives to develop and support high quality provision for their most able pupils. Johanna Raffan is Director of Educational Services at NACE and is one of the three elected delegates representing the UK on the World Council for Gifted and Talented Children.

Renzulli, Joseph

Joseph Renzulli is NEAG Professor for Gifted Education and Talent Development and Director of the National Research Center (USA). His research into the identification of giftedness in pupils and the development of talent in schools has produced the Three Ring Conception of Giftedness, the Enrichment Triad Model and the Schoolwide Enrichment Model (see separate entries). Renzulli identifies two main categories of giftedness:

- *schoolhouse giftedness* – children achieving success in tests and lesson-learning, doing well at school and being readily identified as gifted;
- *creative-productive giftedness* – original thinkers who thrive on research-based and open-ended activities and do not necessarily achieve well at school.

He believes that it is the interaction between these two types of giftedness which best equips a child to fulfil his or her potential. Renzulli promotes the idea that schools should be places for talent development and that all pupils – whatever their test scores – should be given opportunities to achieve their potential. Both he and his wife Sally Reis, Professor of Educational Psychology and Leader Researcher at the NEAG Center, have worked enthusiastically to produce theoretical approaches and practical ideas to support talent development and general school improvement.

Rose, Colin

Colin Rose is Founder and Chairman of Accelerated Learning Systems. He consults and advises many organizations and agencies about thinking and learning, including the DfES. Rose was the main originator of Accelerated Learning (see separate entry) in that he synthesised many earlier ideas of intelligence, thinking skills and learning styles and developed them into Accelerated Learning techniques for use in schools.

S

Smith, Alistair

Alistair Smith is the leading UK trainer in the use of Accelerated Learning techniques in the classroom. He has written a number of books on Accelerated Learning and, together with Nicola Call, wrote *The ALPS Approach* (see ALPS).

Spearman, Charles

Charles Spearman was a British psychologist who was the originator of the two factor theory of intelligence, whereby a combination of G (general intelligence) and S (specific aspects of intelligence) can be used together in various ways to make up the intelligence used in particular situations. S represents aspects of intelligence which can vary in nature and in strength according to the demands of an intellectual task, whereas G is constant for that individual, whatever the activity. Since G is the unchanging factor, Spearman claims that general intelligence (IQ) tests can always give a reasonable prediction of an individual's performance potential in a range of intellectual tasks.

Sternberg, Robert J.

Robert Sternberg is Professor of Psychology and Education at Yale University, USA. He is best known for his study of human intelligence. He published his research findings in *Beyond IQ: A Triarchic Theory of Human Intelligence* (1985). Sternberg's theories have contributed to the rethinking of methods of evaluating an individual's intelligence in order to incorporate practical knowledge. (See Triarchic theory.)

Szabos, Janice R.

Janice Szabos is principal of an elementary school in Virginia, USA. She has conducted action-research across a number of educational fields and is best known for her research into the identification of pupils with high potential. Her practical comparison of the attributes of gifted learners as opposed to those of bright children is used by schools and local education authorities all over the world to distinguish one group from the other.

S

T

Tannenbaum, Abraham J.

Abraham Tannenbaum developed a psychological approach to giftedness, which demonstrates that factors promoting excellence are dependent on individual potential, personal determination and environmental factors, including chance, for example, being in the right place at the right time.

Terman, Lewis

The American, Lewis Terman was the major proponent in the early twentieth century of IQ as an absolute measure of intelligence. In order to substantiate his views, Terman began in 1919 a lifetime study on a sample of scholars who had been identified as having a high IQ. Although he had always believed that intelligence was inherited, fixed and unchanging, he had to revise his views on discovering, as this study unfolded, that there was not a close correlation between IQ scores and adult achievement. He found, indeed, that students with a very high IQ did not necessarily make any mark in science, business, the arts or commerce. This caused Terman to change his position and hold that while high intelligence was a useful and often necessary contribution to success in these spheres in adult life, it was not on its own sufficient. This paradigm was the basis for theories of different types of intelligence and their interrelationships.

Thurstone, Louis Leon

Professor L. L. Thurstone was President of the American Psychological Association and a foremost proponent of a person-centred approach to psychology, suggesting that intelligence is made up of a number of factors. He developed the 'multiple factors' theory, identifying seven primary mental abilities:

- verbal comprehension
- word fluency
- number facility
- spatial visualisation
- associative memory
- perceptual speed
- reasoning.

W

Thurstone also developed ideas about creative thinking and how it can lead to greater flexibility in problem-solving situations, giving, as it does, the ability to consider and evaluate a range of alternative possibilities, without the need to actually experience them. He showed that creativity levels, however, showed little correlation with scores of general intelligence (G) shown in IQ tests.

V

Vygotsky, Lev

Lev Vygotsky, a Russian psychologist, researched and wrote throughout the middle of the twentieth century. He was principally interested in how pupils learn and stressed that they undertake new learning most effectively when they make links with previous learning, thereby transforming their conceptual maps and creating new networks of understanding. Vygotsky also stressed the fundamental role of social learning contexts in individuals' cognitive development, whereby an experienced learner (usually the teacher) models the process for an apprentice learner: 'What a child can do in co-operation today, he can do alone tomorrow.' Vygotsky called this process the 'zone of proximinal development' (see separate entry).

W

Wallace, Belle

Belle Wallace is a freelance lecturer and writer on various aspects of gifted and talented provision and is currently the President of NACE. She spent many years action-researching aspects of thinking skills and problem-solving in various countries, synthesising her own and others' findings to develop her TASC framework (see separate entry) to develop children's thinking and learning skills in the classroom. She has also devised a useful model known as the High Performance Constellation (see separate entry).

Organisations

We have listed below a comprehensive selection of organisations, support groups and funding providers, relating to gifted and talented children, their teachers and their parents in England, Wales, Scotland and Northern Ireland. While most of these groups are based in the UK, we have also included a few major international gifted and talented organisations whose work is relevant in this context.

CONTACT DETAILS

SUPPORT PROVIDED

A

Astronomy.Ac.Uk
Liverpool John Moores University, Twelve Quays House, Egerton Wharf, Birkenhead, CH41 1LD.
Tel: 0151 231 2900
Fax: 0151 231 2921
www.astronomy.ac.uk

Astronomy.Ac.Uk provides astronomy courses by distance learning. These courses can be accessed through three university research institutes and cover a broad range of topics in astronomy.

Away with Maths
Warden's House, Church Lane, Gamlingay, Bedfordshire, SG19 3EX.
Tel: 01767 651196
www.awaywithmaths.com

Away with Maths provides residential maths enrichment weekends for pupils in Years 6, 7 and 8 at various times throughout the school year.

B

BACE
Brunel Able Children's Education Centre, School of Education, Brunel University, 300 St Margaret's Road, Twickenham, Middlesex, TW1 1PT.
Tel: 020 8891 0121 ext. 2070
Fax: 020 8891 8274
www.brunel.ac.uk

BACE offers university-accredited courses for teachers, programmes for gifted pupils, professional development schemes, support for schools and teachers, research reviews and everything to support the understanding of gifted children and their needs.

C

Cambridge Schools Classics Project 3 Ben't Place, Lensfield Road, Cambridge, CV2 1EL.
Tel: 01223 330579 Fax: 0123 322057
www.cambridgescp.com

Provides support for schools and independent learners. Runs Cambridge Online Latin Project for ages 11–16 and Iliad Project for younger pupils.

Center for Talented Youth (CTY) Johns Hopkins University, 3400 N Charles Street, Baltimore, MD 21218, USA.
Tel: (001) 410 516 0337
Fax: (001) 410 516 0804
www.cty.jhu.edu

CTY supports provision for gifted and talented youth through: online courses, information, counselling and advice, research and a magazine for gifted students. Distance learning provision includes challenging courses in writing, maths, ICT and physics.

CHI – Children of High Intelligence 5 Makepeace Avenue, London, N6 6EL.
Tel: 020 8347 8927
www.chi-charity.org.uk

CHI provides consultancy, assessment, liaison, counselling and support for children of exceptional ability (the top 2 per cent), their parents, schools and LEAs. CHI also organises Saturday classes.

D

Duke of Edinburgh Awards Award Head Office, Gulliver House, Madeira Walk, Windsor, Berkshire, SL4 1EU
Tel: 01753 727400
Fax: 01753 810666
www.theaward.org

The Award programme is a flexible non-competitive programme of cultural and adventurous activities available to all young people, aged 14 to 25, whatever their background or ability. There are three levels of award – bronze, silver and gold – which present young people with increasing levels of responsibility and challenge.

Dyslexia Institute
Park House, Wick Road, Egham, Surrey, TW20 0HH.
Tel: 01784 222300 Fax: 01784 222333
www.dyslexia-inst.org.uk

Many dyslexic children are very able. The Dyslexia Institute provides assessment, research, training and support for teachers and parents of gifted and talented children with dyslexia.

E

ECHA –
European Council for High Ability
NACE (National Association for Able Children in Education)
PO Box 242, Arnold's Way, Oxford, OX2 9FR
Tel: 01865 861879
www.ECHA.ws

ECHA promotes awareness of giftedness and talent and acts as a communications network to promote the exchange of information about provision for high ability across Europe.

Exscitec
PO Box 92, Petersfield, Hampshire, GU31 4YF
Tel: 01730 262927 Fax: 01730 268877
www.exscitec.com

Exscitec works with a number of organisations to provide consultancy and support and to develop masterclasses. It also produces written materials related to science, engineering and technology.

G

GIFT
The International Study Centre, Dartford Grammar School, West Hill, Dartford, Kent, DA1 2HW.
Tel/Fax: 01277 654228
www.giftltd.co.uk

GIFT specialises in the education of exceptionally able children and their teachers. It runs residential and non-residential courses, provides advice and training for teachers and produces a range of resources.

H

Headstart and Headstart Focus
Weltech Centre, Ridgeway, Welwyn Garden City, Hertfordshire, AL7 2AA
Tel: 01707 871505 Fax: 01707 322123
www.headstartcourses.org.uk

Headstart is part of the Royal Academy of Engineering's Best programme. It provides intensive four-day residential courses for Year 12 pupils interested in technology-based careers.

I

**Irish Centre for Talented Youth
(CTYI), Dublin City University,**
Dublin 9, Ireland
Tel: 353 1 7005634 Fax: 353 1 7005693
www.dcu.ie/ctyi

CTYI identifies gifted students
through talent searches, providing
Saturday classes, summer schools,
correspondence courses and
Discovery days. CYTI supports
parents and teachers and provides
resources.

M

MDS (Music and Dance Scheme)
DfES Music and Dance Team,
Mowden Hall, Darlington,
Co. Durham, DL3 9BG.
Tel: 01325 391150
www.dfes.gov.uk/mds

This scheme provides financial
support for all or part of the tuition
and boarding fees for exceptionally
talented dancers, musicians and
singers to be able to attend
specialist independent schools,
such as Chethams or the Royal
Ballet School.

MENSA and JUNIOR MENSA
British Mensa Ltd., FREEPOST
(WWW), St John's House, St John's
Square, Wolverhampton WV2 4AH.
Tel: 01902 772771 Fax: 01902 392500
www.mensa.org.uk/junior

Junior Mensa is for children up to
the age of 16 whose IQ is within
the top 2 per cent of the
population. Members are entitled
to belong to two SIGs (Special
Interest Groups). The magazines
Bright Sparks and *Pigasus* are for
Junior Mensans.

N

**NACE – National Association for
Able Children in Education**
PO Box No 242, Arnolds Way,
Oxford, OX2 9FR.
Tel: 01865 861879 Fax: 01865 861880
www.nace.co.uk

NACE provides expertise, advice,
support, consultancy, training,
conferences, events, publications,
newsletters, journals and resources
for teachers of gifted and talented
pupils. It runs development
projects and the Challenge Award
for schools.

**NAGC – National Association for
Gifted Children**, Suite 14,
Challenge House, Sherwood
Drive, Bletchley,
Milton Keynes, MK3 6DP.
Tel: 0870 770 3217 Fax: 0870 770 3219

NAGC provides an education
advisory, information and
counselling service, plus
publications, newsletters and local
support groups for parents of
gifted children. NAGC also runs

www.nagcbritain.org.uk

NAGTY (National Academy for Gifted and Talented Youth)
The University of Warwick, Coventry, CV4 7AL.
Tel: 024 7657 4213 Fax: 024 7657 4221
www.warwick.ac.uk/gifted

NESTA – National Endowment for Science, Technology and the Arts
Fishmongers' Chambers, 110 Upper Thames Street, London, EC4R 3TW.
Tel: 020 7645 9500
www.nesta.org.uk

NPT – National Primary Trust
Westminster College, Oxford, OX2 9AT.
Tel: 01865 245242 Fax: 01865 251847
www.npt.org.uk

P

Potential Trust
Questors 93, The Potential Trust, Shepherd's Close, Kingston Stert, Nr. Chinnor, Oxon., OX9 4NL.

R

ReCAP, The Research Centre for Able Pupils, Westminster Institute of Education, Oxford Brookes University, Harcourt Hill, Oxford, OX2 9AT.
Tel: 01865 488278 Fax: 01865 488393
www.brookes.ac.uk/schools/education/ablepupils

local Saturday classes of stimulating activities for gifted children.

The NAGTY develops, implements, promotes and supports a range of initiatives for gifted and talented children/ students up to 19, provides support for parents/teachers and expertise with which to improve the delivery of gifted and talented education.

NESTA supports and promotes talent, innovation and creativity. It invests in a wide range of people including scientists, inventors, engineers, educators, artists, writers and musicians.

A charity organisation which initiates and funds projects such as Primary Centres and the Children's University, for children between the ages of 3 and 13.

Provides generous funding for a range of projects, initiatives and courses for gifted and talented children.

ReCAP's main work lies in undertaking research relating to gifted and talented education and delivering professional development for teachers, as well as consultancy to schools, LEAs and government bodies.

S

SAPERE
c/o Lizzy Lewis, 51 Lake Street,
Oxford, OX1 4RP.
Tel: 01865 452368
www.sapere.net

SAPERE promotes philosophical enquiry in schools and colleges, organising courses, developing materials and encouraging research. It produces a quarterly newsletter and helps set up local philosophy groups.

SNAP – The Scottish Network for Able Pupils Room 556, St Andrew's Buildings, University of Glasgow, 11 Eldon Street, Glasgow, G3 6NH.
Tel: 0141 330 3071
www.ablepupils.com

SNAP offers support and advice, relating to educators working with gifted and talented children and students in the Scottish education system. It produces a quarterly newsletter and other publications. It also offers support through staff development, national conferences and courses.

Space School UK
National Space Centre, Exploration Drive, Leicester, LE4 5NS.
Tel: 0116 258 2136 Fax: 0116 299 6427
www.spaceschooluk.org

Provides opportunities for KS4 pupils to network with scientists and peers interested in space. Operates a Junior Space School at Easter for younger pupils. Runs the silver CREST award, plus part of the Gold Duke of Edinburgh award.

Smallpeice Trust
Holly House, 74 Upper Holly Walk, Leamington Spa, CV32 4JL.
Tel: 01926 333200 Fax: 01926 333202
www.smallpeicetrust.org.uk

This trust promotes engineering careers to students from Year 9 upwards through residential courses, affiliated to the Royal Academy of Engineering's BEST programme.

Sutton Trust
Heritage House, 21 Inner Park Road, Wimbledon, London, SW19 6ED.
Tel: 020 8788 3223 Fax: 020 8788 3993
www.suttontrust.com

The Sutton Trust funds projects to provide educational opportunities for pupils of non-privileged backgrounds from pre-school to higher education, especially to raise the aspirations of the academically able.

T

Tomorrow's Achievers
Carrington House, 126–130 Regent Street, London, W1B 5EE.
Tel: 020 7734 0161 Fax: 020 7437 1764
www.masterclasses.co.uk

Offers challenging masterclasses and residential courses across a range of subjects and themes across the country for exceptionally able children and students aged from 5–18.

U

UKMT
United Kingdom Mathematics Trust, School of Mathematics, University of Leeds, Leeds, LS2 9JT.
Tel: 0113 343 2339
www.mathcomp.leeds.ac.uk

UKMT aims to advance mathematics education, organising national maths competitions, challenges and enrichment activities for 11–18-year-olds and a forum for teachers. Trains the UK team for the International Mathematical Olympiad.

V

Villiers Park Educational Trust
Royston Road, Foxton, Cambridge, CB2 6SE.
Tel: 01223 872601 Fax: 01223 871640
www.villierspark.org

This trust helps create partnerships between schools, colleges and universities through regional networks and outreach activities, to provide challenging and inspirational opportunities for 14–19-year-olds.

W

World Council for Gifted and Talented Children (WCGTC)
WCGTC Headquarters,
18401 Hiawatha Street, Northridge, CA 91326, USA.
Tel: (001) 818 368 7501
Fax: (001) 818 368 2136
www.worldgifted.org

Dedicated to the needs of gifted and talented children all over the world, the WCGTC has a global network of scholars, teachers, parents, researchers, institutions and others, plus a number of affiliated federations, including NACE and NAGC. Undertakes research and provides a range of services, including publications.

Y

Young Engineers
Chitlee Manor, Liphook,
Hampshire, GU30 7AZ.
Tel: 01428 727265 Fax: 01428 727988
www.youngeng.org.uk

A network of over 1600 UK engineering, science and technology clubs; home to Young Engineer and Junior Engineer Challenge competitions: provides a website for students, teachers and businesses.

Young Enterprise UK
Peterly House, Peterly Road,
Oxford, OX4 2TZ
Tel: 01865 776845 Fax: 01865 775671
www.young-enterprise.org.uk

Offers a range of programmes giving opportunities for students to run real companies and to learn from the first-hand experiences of volunteers. It also runs master-classes in entrepreneurship.

Youth Sport Trust
Sir John Beckwith Centre for Sport,
Loughborough University,
Loughborough, Leicestershire,
LE11 3TU.
Tel: 01509 226600 Fax: 01509 210851
www.youthsports.org

Provides opportunities for talented youngsters in all sports disciplines. Offers various programmes, such as Talent Ladder and Junior Athlete. Organises masterclasses, mentor training and workshops for teachers, pupils and their parents.

Books and Resources

This A–Z section is a comprehensive selection of books and resources to support the teaching and learning of gifted and talented children and to provide background information about the nature of giftedness, intelligence and thinking skills. However, there are many more good books available in addition to those listed here.

Books and resources are divided into three sections:

- reference books and teaching and learning resources
- educational software
- magazines.

Each section is listed alphabetically by author (resources and books) or title (software and magazines).

Reference books and teaching and learning resources

Adey, Philip, Robertson, Anne and Venvill, Grady, *Let's Think: A Programme for Developing Thinking in Five and Six Year Olds*, NFER-Nelson.

Adey, Philip, Serret, Natasha, Robertson, Anne, *et al.*, *Let's Think Through Science*, NFER-Nelson.

Ahmad, Afzal and Williams, Honor, *Numeracy Activities KS2*, Network Educational Press.

Ahmad, Afzal and Williams, Honor, *Numeracy Activities KS3*, Network Educational Press.

Bage, Grant, *Crosslinks* series (various titles), Mill Publishing.

Bell, Barbara, *Minimus: Starting Out in Latin*, Cambridge University Press.

Blagg, Nigel, *et al.*, *Somerset Thinking Skills Course*, Nigel Blagg Associates.

Blinko, Janine and Graham, Noel, *Mathematics with Cubes*, Claire Publications.

Blinko, Janine and Graham, Noel, *Mathematical Beginnings: Problem Solving for Young Children*, Claire Publications.

Bolt, Brian, *Mathematical Activities*, Cambridge University Press.

Bowkett, Stephen, *Imagine That! A Handbook of Creative Activities for the Classroom*, Network Educational Press.

Bowkett, Stephen, *Self-intelligence: A Handbook for Developing Confidence, Self-esteem and Interpersonal Skills*, Network Educational Press.

Bowkett, Stephen, *ALPS StoryMaker*, Network Educational Press.

Bremner, John, *Mensa Maths Genius for Kids*, Carlton Books.

Buxton, Laurie, *Sums for Smart Kids*, BEAM Education.

Buzan, Tony, *The Mindmap Book*, BBC Books.

Caine, Renate Nummela and Caine, Geoffrey, *Mindshifts: A Brain Based Process for Restructuring School and Renewing Education*, Zephyr Press.

Casey, Ron and Koshy, Valsa, *Bright Challenge (KS2)*, Stanley Thornes.

Casey, Ron and Koshy, Valsa, *Bright Challenge: English KS3*, Stanley Thornes.

Caviglioli, Oliver and Harris, Ian, *Mapwise: Accelerated Learning through Visible Thinking*, Network Educational Press.

Caviglioli, Oliver, Harris, Ian and Tindall, Bill, *Thinking Skills and Eye Q*, Network Educational Press.

Chatten, Dave and Skitt, Carolyn, *Mensa Lateral Thinking and Logical Deduction*, Carlton Books.

Chatten, Dave and Skitt, Carolyn, *Mensa Mind Assault Course*, Carlton Books.

CHI, *Gifted and Talented Information Pack*, CHI (see Organisations).

Clark, Catherine and Callow, Ralph, *Educating the Gifted and Talented: Resource Issues and Processes for Teachers*, NACE/Fulton.

Claxton, Guy, *Hare Brain, Tortoise Mind*, Fourth Estate.

Claxton, Guy, *Wise Up*, Network Education Press.

Coates, David and Wilson, Helen, *Challenges in Primary Science*, NACE/Fulton.

Coates, David *et al.*, *Expert Teachers of Able Pupils*, National Primary Trust.

Corrie, Catherine, *Becoming Emotionally Intelligent*, Network Educational Press.

Costello, Patrick, *Thinking Skills and Early Childhood Education*, David Fulton.

Dawes, Lynn, Mercer, Neil and Wegerif, Rupert, *Thinking Together: A Programme of Activities for Developing Thinking Skills at KS2*, Questions Publishing Company.

Dawes, Lynn, Mercer, Neil, Sams, Claire *et al.*, *Talk Box: Activities for Developing Language and Reasoning at KS1*, Questions Publishing Company.

Dean, Geoff, *Challenging the More Able Language User*, NACE/Fulton.

De Bono, Edward, *Mind Pack*, Dorling Kindersley.

De Bono, Edward, *Six Thinking Hats*, Penguin.

De Bono, Edward, CoRT CD-Rom and/or video, www.edwdebono.com

De Bono, Edward, *CoRT Thinking Programme*, Pergamon.

De Bono, Edward, *Teaching Thinking*, Penguin.

De Bono, Edward, *Teach Your Child How to Think*, Penguin.

De Boo, Max, *Nature Detectives*, ASE (Association for Science Education) and the Woodland Trust.

De Boo, Max, *Using Science to Develop Thinking Skills at Key Stage 1: Practical Resources for Teachers*, David Fulton.

Dennison, Paul, *Brain Gym: Teacher's Edition*, Edu-Kinesthetics.

DfES, *Mathematical Challenges for Able Pupils*, DfES.

Dickinson, Chris, *Effective Learning Activities*, Network Educational Press.

Dryden, Gordon and Vos, Jeanette, *The Learning Revolution*, Network Educational Press.

Eyre, Deborah, *Able Children in Ordinary Schools*, NACE/Fulton.

Eyre, Deborah and Lowe, Hilary, *Curriculum Provision for the Gifted and Talented in the Secondary School*, NACE/Fulton.

Eyre, Deborah and McClure, Lynne, *Curriculum Provision for the Gifted and Talented in the Primary School: English, Maths, Science and ICT*, NACE/Fulton.

Fisher, Peter with Wilkinson, Ian, *Thinking through History*, Chris Kington Publishing.

Fisher, Robert, *Teaching Children to Learn*, Nelson Thornes.

Fisher, Robert, *Teaching Children to Think*, Nelson Thornes.

Fisher, Robert, *Games for Thinking*, Nash Pollock Publishing.

Fisher, Robert, *First Poems for Thinking*, Nash Pollock Publishing.

Fisher, Robert, *Poems for Thinking*, Nash Pollock Publishing.

Fisher, Robert, *Stories for Thinking*, Nash Pollock Publishing.

Fisher, Robert, *Values for Thinking*, Nash Pollock Publishing.

Freeman, Joan, *Educating the Very Able: Current International Research*, Ofsted.

Freeman, Joan, *Gifted Children Grown Up*, NACE/Fulton.

Freeman, Joan, Span, Pieter and Wagner, Harald (eds.), *Actualising Talent: A Lifelong Challenge*, www.joanfreeman.com/mainpages/freepapers

Gardner, Howard, *Frames of Mind: The Theory of Multiple Intelligences*, Basic Books.

Gardner, Howard, *Multiple Intelligences: The Theory in Practice*, Basic Books.

Gardner, Howard, *Intelligence Reframed, Multiple Intelligences for the 21st Century*, Basic Books.

Gardner, Howard, *Extraordinary Minds*, Basic Books.

George, David, *The Challenge of the Able Child*, David Fulton.

George, David, *Gifted Education: Identification and Provision*, David Fulton.

George, David and Hughes, Kathryn, *Enrichment Activities for More Able Students*, Chalkface Project.

Gilbert, Ian, *Little Owl's Book of Thinking: An Introduction to Thinking Skills*, Crown House Publishing.

Ginnis, Paul, *The Teacher's Tool Kit: Raise Classroom Achievement with Strategies for Every Learner*, Crown House Publishing.

Glover, Valerie, *Extension Activities in History for More Able Students*, Chalkface Project.

Goleman, Daniel, *Emotional Intelligence: Why It Can Matter More than IQ*, Bloomsbury.

Heimann, Rolf, *Rolf Heimann Puzzle Books*, BEAM Education.

Henshaw, Chris, *Thinking out of the Box*, Available from Incentive Plus.

Higgins, Steve, Baumfield, Viv and Leat, David, *Thinking Through Primary Teaching*, Chris Kington Publishing.

Howe, Michael J. A., *Genius Explained*, Cambridge University Press.

Hughes, Mike, *Closing the Learning Gap*, Network Educational Press.

Hughes, Mike, *Lessons Are for Learning*, Network Educational Press.

Hughes, Mike with Potter, David, *Tweak to Transform: Improving Teaching, a Handbook for School Leaders*, Network Educational Press.

Hughes, Mike with Vass, Andy, *Strategies for Closing the Learning Gap*, Network Educational Press.

Hyams, Sonia M., *Challenges for Children*, Claire Publications.

Hymer, Barry with Michel, Deborah, *Gifted and Talented Learners: Creating a Policy for Inclusion*, NACE/Fulton.

Jackson, Peter, *Mensa Ultimate Puzzle Challenge*, Carlton Books.

Jensen, Eric, *Brain-Based Learning*, The Brain Store.

Jensen, Eric, *Learning with the Body in Mind*, The Brain Store.

Jensen, Eric, *Music with the Brain in Mind*, The Brain Store.

Jensen, Eric, *Super Teaching*, The Brain Store.

Kennard, Roy, *Teaching Mathematically Able Children*, NACE/Fulton.

Kite, Anne, *A Guide to Better Thinking: Teacher's Guide and Pupil's Book*, NFER-Nelson.

Koshy, Valsa, *Teaching Gifted Children 4–7: A Guide for Teachers*, David Fulton.

Koshy, Valsa and Casey, Ron, *Special Ability Scales*, Hodder & Stoughton.

Koshy, Valsa and Murray, Jean, *Unlocking Numeracy*, David Fulton.

Lake, Mike, *Primary Thinking Skills Project Houses and Homes: Brill the Brave*, Questions Publishing Company.

Lake, Mike and Fisher, Frankie, *Improving Thinking Skills through the Literacy Hour*, Questions Publishing Company.

Lake, Mike and Fisher, Frankie, *Primary Thinking Skills Project Personal Development: Brill and the Branikins*, Questions Publishing Company.

Lake, Mike and Needham, Marjorie, *Top Ten Thinking Tactics: Key Stage 2*, Questions Publishing Company.

Lake, Mike, *Primary Thinking Skills Project Weather: Brill and the Riddle of the Whirlwind*, Questions Publishing Company.

Leat, David, *Thinking through Geography*, Chris Kington Publishing.

Lee-Corbin, Hilary and Denicolo, Pam, *Recognising and Supporting Able Children in Primary Schools*, David Fulton.

Leyden, Susan, *Supporting the Child of Exceptional Ability*, NACE/Fulton.

Lucas, Bill and Smith, Alistair, *Help Your Child to Succeed*, Network Educational Press.

Lucas, Bill *et al.*, *Teaching Pupils How to Learn*, Network Educational Press.

Marguiles, Nancy, *Map It!*, Zephyr Press.

McCabe, Mowat A., *Brilliant Activities for Gifted and Talented Children that other Children Will Love Too*, Brilliant Publications.

McGuinness, Carol, *From Thinking Skills to Thinking Classrooms*, DfEE.

Mensa, *Book of Puzzle Challenges*, Dorling Kindersley.

Montgomery, Diane, *Reversing Lower Attainment: Developmental Curriculum Strategies for Overcoming Disaffection and Underachievement*, David Fulton.

Montgomery, Diane, *Gifted and Talented Children with Special Educational Needs: Double Exceptionality*, NACE/Fulton.

Montgomery, Diane, *Able Underachievers*, Whurr Publishing.

Morton, John, *Enrichment Activities for More Able Students 2*, Chalkface Project.

Moser, Adolph, *The Emotional Impact*, Landmark Editions.

Murchison, Joy, *Maths Problems for Gifted and Talented Students*, Claire Publications.

Murris, Karin, *Teaching Philosophy with Picture Books*, Infonet Publications.

Murris, Karin and Haynes, Joanna, *Storywise: Thinking through Stories Key Stages 1 and 2*, Questions Publishing Company.

Naylor, Stuart and Keogh, Brenda, *Concept Cartoons in Science Education*, Millgate House Publishers

O'Brien, Pat, *Teaching Scientifically Able Pupils in the Primary School*, NACE.

O'Brien, Pat, *Teaching Scientifically Able Pupils in the Secondary School*, NACE.

O'Brien, Pat, *Using Science to Develop Thinking Skills at Key Stage 3*, NACE/Fulton.

O'Brien, Tom, *Problems, Challenges and Investigations*, Claire Publications.

Perkins, David, *Smart Schools*, The Free Press.

Pickering, Jon, *Raising Boys' Achievement*, Network Educational Press.

Pomerantz, Michael and Kathryn, Anne, *Listening to Able Underachievers*, NACE/Fulton.

Preston, Henrietta (ed.), *Primary CAME Thinking Maths*, BEAM Education.

Richardson, Carolyn, *Assessing Gifted and Talented Children*, QCA.

Rockett, Mel and Percival, Simon, *Thinking for Learning*, Network Educational Press.

Rose, Colin, *Accelerated Learning*, Accelerated Learning.

Ruff, Ken, *Extension Activities in RE for More Able Students*, Chalkface Project.

Sage, Rosemary, *Class Talk: Successful Learning through Effective Communication*, Network Educational Press.

Salt, Paul, *ICT Projects for High Ability Students*, Chalkface Project.

Sellars, Elaine and Lowndes, Sue, *Using and Applying Mathematics at Key Stage 1*, NACE/Fulton.

Sellars, Elaine and Lowndes, Sue, *Using and Applying Mathematics at Key Stage 2*, NACE/Fulton.

Sellars, Elaine and Lowndes, Sue, *Brain Academy: Numeracy for the More Able Child at Key Stages 1 and 2*, Rising Stars UK Ltd.

Sharon, Howard and Coulter, Martha, *Changing Children's Minds*, Questions Publishing.

Shayer, Michael, Robertson, Anne and Adhami, Mundher, *Let's Think Through Maths*, NFER-Nelson.

Smith, Alistair, *Accelerated Learning in Practice: Brain Based Methods for Accelerating Motivation and Achievement*, Network Educational Press.

Smith, Alistair, *Accelerated Learning in the Classroom*, Network Educational Press.

Smith, Alistair, *The Brains Behind it: New Knowledge about the Brain and Learning*, Network Educational Press.

Smith, Alistair and Call, Nicola, *The Alps Approach: Accelerated Learning in Primary Schools*, Network Educational Press.

Smith, Alistair and Call, Nicola, *The Alps Approach Resource Book*, Network Educational Press.

Snape, Charles and Scott, Heather, *How Puzzling*, Cambridge University Press.

Snape, Charles and Scott, Heather, *How Amazing*, Cambridge University Press.

Sternberg, Robert J., *Thinking Styles*, Cambridge University Press.

Sternberg, Robert J., *Beyond IQ: A Triarchic Theory of Human Intelligence*, Cambridge University Press.

Stopper, Michael J., *Meeting the Social and Emotional Needs of Gifted and Talented Children*, NACE/Fulton.

Sutcliffe, Roger and Williams, Steve, *The Philosophy Club: An Adventure in Thinking*, Questions Publishing Company.

Teare, Barry, *Effective Provision for Able and Talented Children*, Network Educational Press.

Teare, Barry, *Able Pupils: Practical Identification Strategies*, NACE/DfEE.

Teare, Barry, *Challenging Resources for Able and Talented Children*, Network Educational Press.

Teare, Barry, *Effective Resources for Able and Talented Children*, Network Educational Press.

Teare, Barry, *More Effective Resources for Able and Talented Children*, Network Educational Press.

Tilling, Mike, *Adventures in Learning*, Network Educational Press.

Vorderman, Carol, *How Maths Works*, Dorling Kindersley.

Wallace, Belle and Bentley, Richard, *Teaching the Very Able Child: Developing a Policy and Adopting Strategies for Provision*, NACE/Fulton.

Wallace, Belle (ed.), *Teaching Thinking Skills across the Middle Years: A Practical Approach for Children aged 9–14*, NACE/Fulton.

Wallace, Belle (ed.), *Teaching Thinking Skills across the Primary Years: A Practical Approach for All Abilities*, NACE/Fulton.

Wallace, Belle (ed.), *Teaching Thinking Skills Across the Early Years – A Practical Approach for Children aged 4 to 7*, NACE/Fulton.

Wallace, Belle (ed.), *Using History to Develop Thinking Skills at Key Stage 2*, NACE/Fulton.

Walter, Marion, *Make a Bigger Puddle, Make a Smaller Worm*, BEAM Education.

Weatherley, Colin, *Leading the Learning School*, Network Educational Press.

Webb, James T., Meckstroth, Elizabeth A. and Tolan, Stephanie S., *Guiding the Gifted Child: A Practical Source for Parents and Teachers*, Gifted Psychology Press.

Whitworth, Lynda, *Activities to Support Dyslexic High Achievers at Key Stage 3*, Chalkface Project.

Wise, Derek and Lovatt, Mark, *Creating an Accelerated Learning School*, Network Educational Press.

World Class Arena, *Maths Insight* (puzzles and games), www.worldclassarena.org

World Class Arena, *World Class Tests*, www.worldclassarena.org

Educational Software

TITLE	PUBLISHER
Champs	Accelerated Learning Systems
Clay Animation Kit	Tag Learning
Concept Cartoons in Science Education	Milgate House Publishers
Desert Quest	4Mation
Granny's Garden (for early years)	4Mation
Inspiration	Inspiration Software Inc. (available from Tag Learning)
Kidspiration	Inspiration Software Inc. (available from Tag Learning)

Maths Circus Act 3	4Mation
Maths to Win: Games of Strategy	4Mation
Power Maths	Nelson Thornes
Think Maths	BEAM Education
The Tortoise and the Hare: Living Books Series	Tag Learning
Zoombinis Logical Journey (formerly The Mathematical Journey of the Zoombinis)	Mindscape (UK)

Magazines

FOR CHILDREN AND STUDENTS

TITLE	PUBLISHER
Stonesoup (also a website)	www.stonesoup.com
Plus (Internet magazine)	Millennium Mathematics Project, University of Cambridge, www.pass.maths.org
Young Writer	Young Writer, www.mystworld.com/ youngwriter/
Aquila	Aquila, www.aquila.co.uk
Bright Sparks	Junior Mensa (see Organisations)
Pigasus (for younger readers)	Junior Mensa (see Organisations)

FOR TEACHERS

Teaching Thinking	Questions Publishing
G & T Update	Optimus Publishing (Electric Word)
Educating Able Children	NACE

Publishers and Suppliers

This is not intended to be an exhaustive guide to all publishers and suppliers of gifted and talented materials, but rather a source to facilitate contact when seeking to obtain titles which have been listed in the Books and Resources section. Where publishers are imprints of larger publishing groups, the imprint name is given first in this list.

Accelerated Learning Systems Ltd.

50 Aylesbury Road, Aston Clinton, Aylesbury, Bucks, HP22 5AH.
Tel: 01296 631177 Fax: 01296 631074
www.acceleratedlearning.com

- Accelerated Learning books and resources.

Basic Books

387 Park Avenue South, 12th Floor, New York, NY 10016-8810, USA.
Tel: (001) 212 340 8100
www.basicbooks.com

- Non-fiction books by leading intellectuals, academics and journalists.

BBC Consumer Publishing (Books)

BBC Woodlands, 80 Wood Lane, London, W12 0TT.
Tel: 020 8433 2000 Fax: 020 8749 0538
www.bbcshop.com

- The consumer portal for BBC Worldwide.

BEAM Education

Maze Workshops, 72a Southgate Road, London, N1 3JT.
Tel: 020 7684 3323 Fax: 020 7684 3334
www.beam.co.uk

- A specialist in mathematics books, games, and equipment to support teaching and learning across a range of abilities and ages, from 3–14.

Bloomsbury Publishing Plc.

38 Soho Square, London, W1D 3HB.
Tel: 020 7494 2111 Fax: 020 7434 0151
www.bloomsburymagazine.com

- A wide range of fiction and non-fiction books including Daniel Goleman's work on emotional intelligence.

(The) Brain Store, Inc.

4202 Sorrento Valley Boulevard, Ste. B San Diego, CA 92121, USA.
Tel: (001) 800 325 4769 Fax: (001) 858 546 7560
www.thebrainstore.com

- Books and resources related to brain-based learning.

Brilliant Publications

1 Church View, Sparrow Hall Farm, Edlesborough, Dunstable, Bedfordshire, LU6 2ES.
Tel: 01525 229720 Fax: 01525 229725
www.brilliantpublications.co.uk

- A variety of practical activity books across all ability ranges and areas of the curriculum for children aged 10–16.

Buzan Centres Ltd.

54 Parkstone Road, Poole, Dorset, BH15 2PG.
Tel: 01202 674676
www.mind-map.com

- Books, videos and software about mind-mapping techniques.

Cambridge University Press

The Edinburgh Building, Shaftesbury Road, Cambridge, CB2 2RU.
Tel: 01223 312393 Fax: 01223 315052
www.cambridge.org

* A wide range of educational material for all abilities, including *Minimus: Starting out in Latin*.

Carlton Books Ltd.

20 Mortimer Street, London, W1T 3JW.
Tel: 020 7612 0400 Fax: 020 7612 0401
www.carlton.com

* A range of books of 'Mensa' puzzles and challenges.

Chalkface Project

84A High Street, Stony Stratford, Milton Keynes, MK11 1AH.
Tel: 0800 781 8858 Fax: 0845 458 5344
www.chalkface.com

* Online courses and photocopy master lesson plans with worksheets for secondary education. This includes a wide range of materials for gifted and talented children, suitable for upper primary pupils. Free samples can be downloaded.

Chris Kington Publishing

27 Rathmore Road, Cambridge, CB1 7AB.
Tel: 01223 412260 Fax: 01273 240030
www.chriskingtonpublishing.co.uk

* The well-known Thinking Skills series, which includes *Thinking through Geography*.

Claire Publications (also Jonathan Press and Sweet Counter)

Unit 8, Tey Brook Craft Centre, Great Tey, Colchester, CO6 1JE.
Telephone: 01206 211020 Fax: 01206 212755
www.clairepublications.com

* Books relating to problem solving, challenges and investigations.

Crown House Publishing

Crown Buildings, Bancyfelin, Carmarthen, SA33 5ND.
Tel: 01267 211345 Fax: 01267 211882
www.crownhouse.co.uk

- Books on creative teaching and learning.

David Fulton Publishers

The Chiswick Centre, 414 Chiswick High Road, London, W4 5TF.
Telephone: 020 8996 3610 Fax: 020 8996 3622
www.fultonpublishers.co.uk

- A wide range of books and classroom resources to support teachers in all settings. A leading publisher of books for continuing professional development, David Fulton publishes books on gifted and talented education, in partnership with NACE (NACE/Fulton).

DfES Publications

PO Box 5050, Sherwood Park, Annesley, Nottingham, NG15 0DJ.
Tel: 0845 602 2260 Fax: 0845 603 3360
www.dfes.gov.uk/publications

- Government (DfES) documents and guidance.

Dialogue Works

The Old School Business Centre, Newport, SA42 0TS
Tel: 01239 820440
www.dialogueworks.co.uk

- Resources for schools, as well as running a wide variety of courses and projects for developing dialogue and philosophical enquiry.

Dorling Kindersley Limited (Penguin Group UK)

80 Strand, London, WC2R 0RL.
Tel: 020 7010 3000 Fax: 020 7010 6060
www.dk.com

- A range of beautifully illustrated fiction and non-fiction books for all ages.

Edu-Kinesthetics Inc.

PO Box 3395, Ventura, CA93006, USA
Tel: (001) 805 650 3303 Fax: (001) 805 650 1689
www.braingym.com

- Books and manuals about Brain Gym.

4Mation Educational Resources

14 Castle Park Road, Barnstaple, Devon, EX32 8PA.
Tel: 01271 325353 Fax: 01271 322974
www.4Mation.co.uk

- Educational software, including challenges, problems and simulations.

Fourth Estate

HarperCollins Publishers, 77-85 Fulham Palace Road, London W6
8JB.
Tel: 020 8741 7070 Fax: 020 8307 4440
www.fireandwater.com

- A wide range of educational books.

Free Press

Simon & Schuster, Africa House, 64-78 Kingsway, London, WC2B
6AH.
Tel: 020 7316 1900 Fax: 020 7316 0331/2
www.simonsays.co.uk

- Science and education books.

Gifted Psychology Press

Great Potential Press, PO Box 5057, Scottsdale, AZ 85261, USA.
Tel: (001) 602 954 4200 Fax: (001) 602 954 0185
www.giftedbooks.com

- Specialist publishers of books relating to psychology and gifted
  education.

Hodder & Stoughton

338 Euston Road, London, NW1 3BH.
Tel: 020 7873 6000 Fax: 020 7873 6024
www.hodderheadline.co.uk and www.hoddertests.co.uk

- A wide variety of genres, including educational books and cognitive ability tests.

Incentive Plus

PO Box 5220, Great Horwood, Milton Keynes, MK17 0YN.
Tel: 01908 526120 Fax: 01908 526130
www.incentiveplus.co.uk

- A wide range of books, videos, posters, games, CD-ROMs and other resources on teaching gifted and talented children, multiple intelligences, emotional literacy and behaviour management.

Infonet Publications

JISC Executive, King's College London, Strand Bridge House, 138-142 The Strand, London, WC2R 1HH.
Tel: 020 7848 2937 Fax: 020 7848 2939
www.jisc.ac.uk

- A small selection of books, mainly related to higher education.

Inspiration Software Inc.

7412 SW Beaverton-Hillsdale Hwy, Suite 102, Portland, OR 97225, USA
Tel: (001) 503 297 3004 Fax: (001) 503 297 4676
www.inspiration.com

- Develops and publishes innovative software tools to support the development of visual learning, thinking and organisational skills.

Landmark Editions

PO Box 270169, 1402 Kansas Avenue, Kansas City, Missouri 64127, USA.
Tel: (001) 800 653 2665 Fax: (001) 816 483 3755
www.landmarkeditions.com

- Books for students by students, including the *Emotional Impact* series.

Lucky Duck Publishing

Solar House, Station Road, Kingswood, Bristol, BS15 4PH.
Telephone: 0117 947 5150 Fax: 0117 947 5152
www.luckyduck.co.uk

- Books, videos and training materials for all age groups, across a range of topics including thinking skills, self-esteem, emotional literacy and behaviour management.

Millgate House Publishers (The ConCISE Project)

Millgate House, 30 Mill Hill Lane, Sandbach, Cheshire, CW11 4PN.
Tel/Fax: 01270 764314
www.conceptcartoons.com

- A small independent publishing company set up to make Concept Cartoons more widely available. Resources in a number of formats, including posters, science story books, CD-ROMs and photocopiable materials.

Mill Publishing

PO Box 120, Bangor, Co. Down, BT19 7BX.
Tel: 0800 731 2837 Fax: 0800 027 2833
www.millpublishing.co.uk

- The *Crosslinks* series of cross-curricular thinking skills materials. (Free materials downloadable from the website.)

Mindscape (UK) Limited

Gainsborough House, 28-32 High Street, Crawley, RH10 1BW.
www.mindscape.co.uk

- Educational software.

NACE/Fulton

NACE National Office, PO Box 242, Arnolds Way, Oxford, OX2 9FR.
Tel: 01865 861879 Fax: 01865 861880
www.nace.co.uk

- A range of books for teachers, relating to gifted and talented education and thinking skills, in partnership with David Fulton Publishers (see separate entry).

Nash Pollock

York Publishing Services, 64 Hallfield Road, Layerthorpe, York, YO3 7XQ.
Tel: 01904 431213 Fax: 01904 430868
www.yps-publishing.co.uk

- A range of books – including those by Robert Fisher – to support the teaching of thinking skills.

Nelson Thornes Ltd.

Delta Place, 27 Bath Road, Cheltenham, Gloucester, GL53 7TH.
Tel: 01242 267100 Fax: 01242 221914
www.nelsonthornes.com

- A variety of educational books, software, and online resources for all ability ranges, including titles for gifted and talented pupils.

Network Educational Press

PO Box 635, Stafford, ST16 1BF.
Tel: 01785 225515 Fax: 01785 228566
www.networkpress.co.uk

- Books and materials to support the teaching of gifted and talented children – a comprehensive website with clear descriptions of resources.

NFER-Nelson Publishing Co Ltd.

The Chiswick Centre, 414 Chiswick High Road, London, W4 5TF.
Tel: 0845 6021937 Fax: 020 8996 3660
www.nfer-nelson.co.uk

- Tests, assessments and training, consultancy, health and education materials across a range of abilities.

Nigel Blagg Associates

Grove House, 39 Staplegrove Road, Taunton, Somerset, TA1 1DG.
Tel: 01823 336204

- Publishes the *Somerset Thinking Skills* Course

Ofsted

Ofsted Publications Centre
Tel: 07002 637833 Fax: 07002 693274
www.ofsted.gov.uk

- A wide range of documents and reports.

Optimus Publishing

Electric Word plc, 67-71 Goswell Road, London EC1V 7EP.
Tel: 020 7251 9034 Fax: 020 7251 9045
www.optimuspub.co.uk

- *G & T Update* – a magazine for Gifted and Talented Co-ordinators – ten times per year.

Penguin

80 Strand, London, WC2R 0RL.
Tel: 020 7010 3000 Fax: 020 7010 6060
www.penguin.co.uk

- A wide range of books related to education.

Pergamon

Elsevier Science Ltd., The Boulevard, Langford Lane, Kidlington, Oxford, OX5 1GB.
Tel: 01865 843000 Fax: 01865 843010
www.books.elsevier.com

- Science and technology books, including educational psychology.

(The) Questions Publishing Company Ltd.

Leonard House, 321 Bradford Street, Digbeth, Birmingham B5 6ET.
Tel: 0121 666 7878 Fax: 0121 666 7879
www.education-quest.com

- Produces the *Teaching Thinking* magazine as well as other books and materials to support the teaching of gifted and talented children.

Rising Stars UK Ltd.

76 Farnaby Road, Bromley, Kent, BR1 4BH.
Tel: 020 8313 0191

- Curriculum resources, especially mathematics.

SAGE Publications Ltd.

1 Oliver's Yard, 55 City Road, London EC1Y 1SP.
Tel: 020 7324 8500 Fax: 020 7324 8600
www.sagepub.co.uk

- Books on teaching and learning issues related to gifted and talented pupils.

Stanley Thornes

See entry for Nelson Thornes.

Tag Learning

25 Pelham Road, Gravesend, Kent, DA11 0HU.
Tel: 01474 357350 Fax: 01474 537887
www.taglearning.com

- Educational software, peripherals, training and support materials.

Whurr Publications Ltd.

19b Compton Terrace, London, N1 2UN.
Telephone: 020 7359 5979 Fax: 020 7226 5290
www.whurr.co.uk

- Books and journals on special needs, including for those also with gifts or talents. Specialises in books on dyslexia for teachers and parents.

Zephyr Press

814 N. Franklin Street, Chicago, Illinois 60610, USA.
Tel: (001) 800 232 2187 Fax: (001) 312 337 5985
www.zephyrpress.com

- Books on multiple intelligences, thinking skills and teaching and learning.

Websites

Here is a selection of websites which provide useful information, support, challenges, resources and links relating to gifted and talented provision. Many of the sites are general, while others are subject-specific. For some, the audience is definitely the children themselves, or teachers or parents; others include all three. In order to make it easier for you to find what you want, we have identified audience and category/subject against each site. All details are correct at the time of printing, but websites frequently change or close, so check the directories for new alternatives. Happy surfing!

Key to websites

Audience

Ch	Children
P	Parents
T	Teachers

Categories

AD	Art and Design
C	Cross-curricular
D	Directory
DT	Design Technology
G	General
Geo	Geography and the Environment
H	History
ICT	Information Communication Technology
L	Literacy
Lat	Latin and the Classics
M	Maths

MFL	Modern Foreign Languages
Mu	Music
O	Other, including challenges, puzzles, games and competitions
PE	Physical Education
Ph	Philosophy
R	RE
S	Science
Th	Thinking Skills

Audience

Ch	T	P	Websites	Category
	•		www.1000problems.com Ready-made maths problems for teachers of gifted children to download for classroom use.	M
•	•		www.accessart.org.uk Very good animated site with stimulating visual arts learning resources, online workshops and interactive arts for children, plus ideas for teachers to extend thinking skills through arts projects.	AD Th
	•		www.archive.official-documents.co.uk Ofsted review of research: 'Educating the Very Able' (enter this title in the search window then download).	G
•			www.artattack.co.uk Art Attack – examples from broadcast programmes and instructions for making artworks, for all ages.	AD
•			www.bbc.co.uk/education/languages Provides opportunities for students of languages to learn at their own pace, using online courses in a range of languages, including fast-track challenges.	MFL
•			www.booktrust.org/uk This site runs book prizes, projects and opportunities to write book reviews to encourage readers of all ages to enjoy books.	L

Audience Ch T P	Websites	Category
• •	www.brookes.ac.uk/go/cpdgifted/ A UK open access website sponsored by the DfES, containing a range of gifted and talented CPD and informational material for a wide range of audiences.	G
• •	www.cambridgescp.com Cambridge School Classics Project. Online Latin course, teaching and learning resources and information, classical myths activities and performance storytelling.	Lat
•	www.case-network.org Cognitive Acceleration through Science Education website – information and support for teachers.	S
• •	www.coolmath.com A fun American maths and science website for all ages, with games and puzzles, including an 'amusement park of math'.	M S O
• •	www.counton.org A UK site for children keen on interactive maths games and investigations, plus resources, a monthly MathZine and an index for teachers.	M G O
•	www.cut-the-knot.com A site offering a range of interactive maths puzzles and activities for all ages.	M O
•	www.dialogueworks.co.uk Training, articles, ideas and resources for developing children's citizenship thinking skills and social confidence, plus philosophy for children.	Th Ph
•	http://dir.yahoo.com/Education/k_12/gifted_youth/ Comprehensive listings of links to gifted and talented websites, worldwide.	D

Audience Ch	T	P	Websites	Category
	•		http://education.massey.ac.nz Enter 'gifted education' in search window. Very useful New Zealand site providing information and links to resources, support, school-based initiatives, discussion groups and useful websites across the world.	G D
	•	•	http://ericec.org/gifted.html Worldwide links to many organisations, resources, magazines and discussion groups relating to gifted and talented provision.	D
•			www.eskimo.com/~billb/ The Science Hobbyist site. A great website with all kinds of options from 'cool science' to 'weird science'! Lots of ideas for experiments and projects.	S
•	•	•	www.funbrain.com Everything zany and fun to stimulate and challenge, from games such as 'Maths Baseball' and 'Grammar Gorillas' to daily Funbrain journals, plus sections for teachers and parents too.	C G O
	•		www.geocities.com/ljkaiser_1823 Michigan Alliance for Gifted Education. Masses of brilliant links and ideas for gifted students and for teachers of gifted children, from Early Years upwards.	G
•			www.germanfortravellers.com A practical site for those learning German, with links to media and shopping, plus chat and pen-pals.	MFL
•	•	•	www.gifteddevelopment.com/links.htm US site with great links for gifted children, parents and teachers – everything from killer whales to chess!	G C D
•			www.greenpeace.org A lively ecology site with opportunities to join discussions on ecology issues.	Geo S L

Audience				
Ch	T	P	Websites	Category
•			www.hhmi.org/coolscience 'Cool Science for Curious Kids' – various biology activities such as 'classifying critters' or 'air junk'.	S
		•	www.hoagiesgifted.org/parents.htm Helpful American site providing information and support for parents of gifted children.	G
	•		www.hoagiesgifted.org/investigations.htm Thousands of ideas and lesson-plans for investigations across the curriculum for gifted and talented pupils of all ages, plus free online language courses and many other useful links.	C MFL
•			www.hoagiesgifted.org/hoagies_kids.htm Lots of interactive options for gifted children and teenagers, including reading lists, movies, magazines, contests, software reviews and children's own contributions (various, including art and poetry).	L AD G
	•		www.hoagiesgifted.org/educators.htm A plethora of support, advice and ideas for teaching gifted and talented children.	G
	•		www.ictadvice.org.uk Enter 'gifted and talented' in search window to find comprehensive advice about using ICT for teaching gifted and talented children, plus list of useful websites and a resource exchange.	ICT G D
	•		www.intuitivemedia.com/talentladder Advice, guidance and information links for primary and secondary teachers of sports-talented pupils, with links to a number of talent-development initiatives.	PE
•			www.justthink.org A good site for young people interested in the media, media literacy, production and creating media messages – offers media workshops for young people.	AD Th G

Audience				
Ch	T	P	Websites	Category

•		•	www.kidspsych.org A great interactive site. Games for ages 1–9 to develop cognitive thinking, spatial memory and deductive reasoning, plus information for parents.	Th O G
	•		www.literacytrust.org.uk A useful site with a gifted children's page.	L
•	•		www.maryrose.org Interactive site to explore life on board the Tudor ship, the *Mary Rose*.	H
•	•		www.mathcomp.leeds.ac.uk A range of maths challenges and enrichment activities for children.	M
•			www.mathsnet/into.html A site for children, offering a range of maths games, puzzles, facts and also an online chess club.	M O
	•		www.mathsphere.co.uk A site for teachers of gifted and talented children, providing lesson plans, resources, games, puzzles and software reviews.	M O
•			www.mathsyear 2000.org Although Maths year is long past, this site is still going strong with a range of maths games, puzzles and curiosities for all ages.	M O
	•		www.nace.co.uk The National Association for Able Children in Education's website, to support teachers and schools, providing information, advice, resources, consultancy, training, research and development updates and details of the Challenge Award.	G
		•	www.nagcbritain.org.uk The National Association for Gifted Children's website, to support parents.	G

Audience				
Ch	T	P	Websites	Category

•			www.nagcbritain.org.uk/activities/youth.html Youth Café. Children's own part of the NAGC website, with various interactive options.	G
	•		www.nagcbritain.org.uk/activities/menuteachers.html Teachers' Bistro. Teachers' part of the NAGC website, with everything regarding provision for gifted and talented children, including research, support, resources and ideas for middle and secondary schoolteachers.	G
•			www.naturegrid.org.uk/infant An interactive science website for younger children, including interactive big books, several of them with Welsh language versions and one in French. Children can email their pictures and letters for the pin-board.	S L MFL
	•		www.ncaction.org.uk Useful site for National Curriculum assessment and extension of children's work – all subjects and all ages.	G
	•		www.nc.uk.net/gt National Curriculum guidance on teaching gifted and talented children, advice regarding all aspects of gifted and talented provision, case studies and links to a wide range of subject-specific teaching resources and organisations.	G D
•			www.nhm.ac.uk/interactive/kids/index.html The National History Museum's interactive area 'for kids', with projects and games to become real scientists and natural historians and links to the museum's main site.	S H O
•			www.nrich.org.uk The online maths enrichment site run by Cambridge University, offering maths challenges for very able mathematicians of all ages.	M O

Audience			Websites	Category
Ch	T	P		

| | | | www.nysed.gov/ciai/gt/gift/arts/arts1.htm | |
| • | | | The New York State Education Department's site to help identify artistic or musical talent and to offer units of work, activities, resources and links to other sites. | AD M G |

| | | | www.oagc.com/gtinternetsites.htm | |
| • | | | Ohio Association for Gifted Children. Loads of links and resources for teachers of gifted and talented children (including many to pass on to parents and children), together with brief review summaries of each. | G |

| | | | www.playmusic.org | |
| • | | | An interactive site with a 'kidzone' to find out all about the orchestra through its different sections. | M |

| | | | www.qca.org.uk/2623.html | |
| • | | | This is the area of the QCA (Qualifications and Curriculum Authority) website which gives details of optional extension tasks for pupils in Key Stage 2. | L M S |

| | | | www.science-active.co.uk | |
| • | | | Science Active site intended for secondary and college students, including animations and interactive quizzes. | S |

| | | | www.sciencemuseum.org.uk | |
| • | • | | Science Museum activities and ideas for teachers and pupils, plus a login point for children, including the facility to create their own personal websites. | S O |

| | | | www.sciencenet.org.uk/index.html | |
| • | | | Lots of sections to choose from, such as archaeology and palaeontology, medicine, astronomy or psychology, to gain information, book reviews, careers advice, interviews with scientists and links to other sites. | S |

Audience Ch T P	Websites	Category
•	www.shodor.org/ssep/index.html Interactive 'Student Science Enrichment Programme'. Creative science, including interactive games and activities for gifted children.	S O
• •	www.sosmath.com/index.html More than 2,500 pages of maths activities (all aspects) for gifted children of all ages.	M
•	www.standards.dfes.gov.uk/giftedandtalented/ Guidance to teachers of gifted and talented children and information regarding the latest developments, conferences, resources, training, examples of good practice and discussion forums.	G
•	www.stonesoup.com Stimulating website for 8–13-year-olds, inviting them to contribute writing (stories, poems, articles, reviews) and artwork to their own magazine.	L AD G
•	www.stories.com Writing.Com's online community for all ages of writers and readers.	L
•	www.storiesfromtheweb.org An interactive magazine site for readers and young writers aged 8-14.	L
•	www.teachernet.gov.uk Enter 'gifted and talented' in search window. A DfES website, providing information and articles about teaching gifted and talented children.	G
•	http://teachingtreasures.com/au Australian site with hundreds of ideas, lesson plans and resources for teaching gifted and talented children from Foundation Stage to the end of KS3.	G

Audience				
Ch	T	P	Websites	Category

•			www.teachingthinking.net Robert Fisher's site for teachers about thinking skills – ideas and resources for the classroom.	Th
•			www.teachspace.org A teacher resource project at the California Space and Science Center, with lots of useful links.	S
•			www.telescope.org An interactive site, with opportunities to use the Bradford robotic telescope and learn about topics like astronomy, the weather and particle physics.	S Geo
•			www.terry-deary.com Interactive, fun website from the author of the Horrible Histories series – includes a ghoulish mystery game.	H L O
•			www.tki.org.nz Useful New Zealand site. Select English language, then go to 'search' and select 'gifted and talented' to choose aspects from a long list of gifted and talented issues for helpful ideas and information.	G
•			www.tornadoproject.com A fascinating exploration of US tornadoes, including updates, stories, storm-chasing and curiosity corner.	Geo L
•			www.volcano.und.nodak.edu An interesting US website with updates on current eruptions, volcanic simulations, games and fun stuff.	Geo
•	•	•	www.vsg.edu.au Virtual School for the Gifted – an online 'school', providing enrichment courses to challenge able students at home or at school, plus an online community and discussion forum (based in Australia, but with worldwide audience).	G O

Audience			Websites	Category
Ch	T	P		
•	•	•	www.worldclassarena.org The site to find out about international World Class Tests in maths and problem-solving.	M O
	•		www.xcalibre.ac.uk This excellent DfES-supported website is a subject-specific source of guidance and a directory of educational resources and links for teachers of gifted and talented pupils in the 4–19 age range.	G D
•	•		www.youngeng.org Website for youngsters who enjoy design technology and might be considering engineering as a career. It presents information about science, engineering and technology clubs around the UK, details of a range of challenges, competitions and events, plus teaching resources for schools.	DT S